"This is the book I sorely needed when I began my teaching career. It's easy to imagine the relief and support both brand-new and early career teachers will feel when reading *Real Talk for New Teachers*. Bishop and Farber address topics that teacher education programs do not necessarily have time to address, ones that become immediately crucial in the early years of the teaching profession."

—*Dr. Valerie Bang-Jensen,* Author of *Literacy Moves Outdoors: Learning Approaches for Any Environment*

"This book is so relatable on so many levels. As a first-year teacher, I have left some days exhausted, in defeat, even in tears. This book not only acknowledged my feelings, but offered helpful strategies from people that have actually been through it, and know exactly how I am feeling."

—*Jenna Hitchen,* first-year teacher

"*Real Talk for New Teachers* is a MUST for anyone entering the teaching field or in their first years of teaching! This book makes teaching feel 'doable' in a holistic manner that starts with the self (living healthily) and moves toward collaborating with others and becoming a leader in the profession."

—*Dr. Stacy Simonyi,* Assistant Professor of Education, Saint Michael's College

Real Talk for New Teachers

Real Talk for New Teachers helps beginning teachers develop their vision and orient their practice toward a personally fulfilling, healthy, and sustainable career.

Having a sustainable career goes beyond buzzwords like self-care, and Farber and Bishop provide meaningful ideas for balancing the demands of the profession and getting the most out of it. Topics include managing health, time, and emotions; building community with students and families; collaborating with colleagues; creating an engaging curriculum; and leading a busy classroom.

Each chapter features loads of practical strategies, an approachable, encouraging tone, helpful inspirations, useful resources, space to write and reflect, and, most importantly, guidance to help you develop a personal action plan. Whether you read this book alone or with a mentor, you'll come away with clear ways to cultivate strong learning communities and practices that support both personal and collective efficacy in this vital profession.

Dr. Katy Farber is an Assistant Professor of Education at Saint Michael's College. She has over 25 years of education experience, including as a teacher and a professional development coordinator. Katy has authored or co-authored six books, regularly writes for educational journals and websites, and presents at conferences. Read more about her work at katyfarber.com.

Dr. Penny Bishop is Dean of Boston University Wheelock College of Education and Human Development. A former middle grades teacher, Penny has spent two decades researching effective school environments and teaching middle grades educators. This is her eighth co-authored book in the field of education.

Also Available from Routledge Eye on Education
(www.routledge.com/k-12)

The Student Motivation Handbook:
50 Ways to Boost an intrinsic Desire to Learn
Larry Ferlazzo

Passionate Learners, 3e:
How to Engage and Empower Your Students
Pernille Ripp

What Great Teachers Do Differently:
Nineteen Things That Matter Most
Todd Whitaker

Classroom Management from the Ground Up
Todd Whitaker, Katherine Whitaker, Madeline Good

Teaching with a Strength-Based Approach:
How to Motivate Students and Build Relationships
Steven Barron

Scaffolding for Success:
Helping Learners Meet Rigorous Expectations
Across the Curriculum
Barbara R. Blackburn

Real Talk for New Teachers

Tools for Building a Sustainable Career

Katy Farber and Penny Bishop

Routledge
Taylor & Francis Group
NEW YORK AND LONDON

Designed cover image: Getty Images

First published 2025
by Routledge
605 Third Avenue, New York, NY 10158

and by Routledge
4 Park Square, Milton Park, Abingdon, Oxon, OX14 4RN

Routledge is an imprint of the Taylor & Francis Group, an informa business

© 2025 Katy Farber and Penny Bishop

The right of Katy Farber and Penny Bishop to be identified as authors of this work has been asserted in accordance with sections 77 and 78 of the Copyright, Designs and Patents Act 1988.

All rights reserved. No part of this book may be reprinted or reproduced or utilised in any form or by any electronic, mechanical, or other means, now known or hereafter invented, including photocopying and recording, or in any information storage or retrieval system, without permission in writing from the publishers.

Trademark notice: Product or corporate names may be trademarks or registered trademarks, and are used only for identification and explanation without intent to infringe.

ISBN: 9781032847405 (hbk)
ISBN: 9781032823379 (pbk)
ISBN: 9781003514725 (ebk)

DOI: 10.4324/9781003514725

Typeset in Palatino
by codeMantra

This book is dedicated to every single new and beginning teacher. We believe in you and want you to THRIVE in this dynamic and fulfilling career.

Contents

Acknowledgments   x
Meet the Authors   xi
Letter from the Authors   xiii
How to Use This Book   xv

1 **Living Healthily**   1

2 **Managing Time**   13

3 **Managing Emotions**   31

4 **Collaboration with Your School Community**   44

5 **Building Meaningful Curriculum**   54

6 **Building Community with Students**   70

7 **Building Community with Families**   81

8 **Leading a Busy Classroom**   92

9 **Pulling It All Together**   106

Afterword: Becoming a Teacher Leader   118
References   122

Acknowledgments

We would like to acknowledge the many teachers who took the time to offer their words of wisdom for new teachers. They are the heart and soul of this book.

Meet the Authors

Dr. Katy Farber has over 25 years of education experience, including 19 years as a teacher and teacher leader, and 5 as a professional development coordinator at the University of Vermont's Tarrant Institute for Innovative Education. She has conducted research about adolescent education and service learning, and partnered with schools to help them personalize learning, engage students, and participate in action research.

She is an Assistant Professor at Saint Michael's College, co-directs the Middle Grades Collaborative and the Teaching and Learning program at the Institute for the Environment. She has authored or co-authored four books about education, including *Why Great Teachers Quit and How We Might Stop the Exodus*, *Real and Relevant: a guide to service and project-based learning*, *Change the World with Service Learning*, and *Personalized Learning in the Middle Grades*. Katy regularly writes for educational websites and journals, presents at state and national conferences, and collaborates with teachers. She works to elevate the voices of students and teachers and advocates for teacher and student leadership, authentic learning and deep, powerful service for others and the natural world.

She lives in central Vermont with her husband and two daughters and loves being outside with family and friends, listening to music, and jumping into Vermont ponds and lakes.

Dr. Penny A. Bishop is Dean of Boston University Wheelock College of Education & Human Development and a professor of teaching and learning. Prior to this, she was a professor of education at the University of Vermont and Dean at the University of Maine. A scholar of early adolescence and middle grades education and former middle school teacher, Penny has published seven earlier books on education, including *The Successful Middle School: This We Believe* (AMLE); *Personalized Learning in the Middle Grades* (Harvard Education Press); and *Reaching and Teaching Middle Grades Learners* (Corwin Press). She has also published dozens of widely cited book chapters and articles in top peer-reviewed journals.

Penny's research, which focuses on providing responsive learning environments for young adolescents, has garnered more than $13 million in external support from public and foundation sources, and she has received several major honors for her work, including the John H. Lounsbury Award for Distinguished Achievement in Middle Level Education from the Association for Middle Level Education and the James P. Garvin Distinguished Service Award from the New England League of Middle Schools. Her global engagement work includes serving as a Sir Ian Axford Fellow at New Zealand's Ministry of Education and the establishment of two international programs for preservice and practicing educators and leaders.

Penny lives in the Boston area with her husband and very naughty dog, Tally.

Letter from the Authors

Welcome to our beautifully laid, cozy, dining table. It is long and well-worn, and has been visited by the thousands of teachers who came before you. This time, however, we have laid a place setting for *you*. Pull up a chair and let's talk.

First of all, thank you for joining us. The fact that you picked up this book suggests that you're embarking upon some of the world's most impactful work – educating our next generation. You are nurturing the development of the world's children and youth. What could be more important?

Maybe you're just beginning this new career or perhaps you've been at it a little while already. Perhaps you're eager to be in the classroom. You might also be feeling a little nervous. Here's the thing. It's ok to feel both ways. Teaching is a *both-and* profession. It is *both* extraordinary *and* exhausting. It is both joyful and underappreciated. Rejuvenating and draining. Creative and mundane. This is the lifelong dichotomy of being a teacher. It is both the challenge and the opportunity of teaching.

Teaching can be hard to sustain. We've seen many teachers burn out and that's why we decided to write this book. To let new teachers know that there are proven ways to embrace the opportunities while managing the challenges. It seems everything we read or see lately suggests that the solution to the problem of teacher burnout is "self-care." This often comes with a suggestion that a candle, a bath, and a cup of tea will fix everything. (Spoiler alert: They won't, although sometimes they don't hurt.) Instead, we humbly suggest that you will need to be intentional about leading a healthy life, managing your emotional and mental health, collaborating with colleagues, students, and families, and investing in powerful pedagogies, among other things.

Throughout our careers, we reflect, learn, and grow. We also need to rest, recover, and rejuvenate. Both research and personal experience tell us that educators who sustain, those who stay in this amazing profession we call teaching, find strategies to not only survive, but to thrive. They figure out not only to persevere now but to do so joyfully. And that's what we hope to share with you: research, personal experience, and strategies for sustaining. Because we need you. We need you to teach our children, to model for our children, and, yes, to love our children.

We join you at this dining table as educators who've learned a few things from our own struggles. Some of these struggles were the same as you'll face, and some will be different. Regardless, we want to help you make teaching a sustainable career. Because the work of educating the next generation is essential. YOU are essential. We need you to be healthy, and to feel a sense of pride and fulfillment in working with our children and youth. We hope this book will help you shape a long future in this amazing, creative, and wonderful field of education.

Welcome to the table. We are so glad you are here.

How to Use This Book

We've designed this book to be interactive. Over the course of engaging with it, you'll come away with several things. The knowledge that you're not alone. Pearls of wisdom from veteran teacher-colleagues. Inspiration from stories of success. And, most importantly, a personal plan.

Your plan will change over time because *you* will change. But you'll have a great start and you will have identified the support to help you along your journey.

We've chosen to use the first-person plural "we" in this book because we wrote it together. I (Katy) draw upon my 19 years of experience as a public school teacher, most recently teaching fifth grade in a rural school during the COVID-19 pandemic. I also worked as a professional development coordinator with teachers across the state of Vermont, and I'm now an assistant professor helping pre-service teachers launch their own journeys to the classroom. I (Penny) began my career as a middle school teacher before becoming a teacher educator, working with hundreds of pre- and in-service teachers and studying what works in education. Together, we've drawn from a wide community of practicing and retired teachers who have contributed insights to this book, educators who generously offered their input and advice for you.

We also want to acknowledge that as two middle-aged white women, our lens, writing, and advice may not resonate with you. That is okay. We hope that through the research, the quotes from other teachers, and the many resources here, you will find something that does resonate with you and you can take into your practice. Also, new teachers, like any group of people, are not a monolith. Each one will have a different experience, but there are some commonalities likely for those new to teaching. These are what we present in this book.

Each chapter has the following sections:

- Overview (what this chapter is about)
- Connect (an example from practice)
- Real Talk (real talk about what works)
- Dig Deeper (additional resources)
- Reflect, Dream, Plan (space to imagine plans and solutions)
- Identify Your Big Three (your action steps for a sustainable profession)

We know that you might not want or need to use the whole book. That is also okay. Just use the parts you need, as you need them. We believe in student (and teacher!) choice, differentiation, agency, and engagement, so use this book however you see fit. The short of it is, we believe in you. And there is always a spot for you at our table.

PERMISSION SLIP

YOU ARE HEREBY GRANTED PERMISSION TO:
- READ THIS BOOK IN ANY ORDER
- SKIP SECTIONS THAT DO NOT SPEAK TO YOU
- DEVOUR THIS BOOK IN ONE SITTING
- TAKE ALL YEAR TO READ THIS BOOK
- DRAW ALL OVER THE PAGES

1

Living Healthily

Chapter Overview

This chapter is not here to make healthy living another thing on your "to do" list. Instead, we want you to understand how making your own mental and physical health a priority enables you to be the kind of powerful educator (and person!) we know you want to be. First, we'll explore how self-care has been marketed to us as if we need to BUY something to achieve healthy living. We will explore the myths around work and the societal context we live in, and how these impact teachers. Next, we'll sort through the actual ideas that help, with insights from veteran teachers, and a few ideas from current research on sleep, rest, and stress. Finally, you'll think about your own plan for healthy living while teaching.

Connect

Teaching during the COVID-19 pandemic brought a specific kind of urgency to focusing on mental health for many educators. Most of us faced a new level of uncertainty each day. Which safety protocols would be in existence? Which would have changed? Which students or colleagues would be sick or absent? What were the implications of those absences?

For Katy, who was teaching fifth grade during the pandemic, these uncertainties felt overwhelming at times. She realized she needed to get really clear about her

DOI: 10.4324/9781003514725-1

healthy living practices. For her, they became life rafts, providing a kind of sanity in a day full of uncertainty. This meant making time for herself, and that meant getting up early. Before anyone in her family was awake and needed things. Needed her! Each morning, she rose early and began the day in a calm way, sacrificing a little sleep in order to do so. She drank her first cup of coffee on the couch in silence. Then she meditated for about ten minutes, gently noticing her thoughts and regulating her breath.

Our friend Ally also chose to get up early. Her life raft, however, was working out. As a busy mom of very young children, she juggled constant childcare closures while teaching during the pandemic. Ally would ride her stationary bike or do a workout video every day before school. It was inspiring! She also defined a hard boundary of leaving right after school to do the afternoon pickup and childcare.

Jorge, a third-year teacher and avid bass player, relied on his music. He knew that what brought him joy was the feeling of being lost in the moment. He leveraged online platforms to play with his bandmates virtually, a way to do this despite the quarantine. He protected his Thursday nights and organized his time for instructional planning and assessment around that.

Katy's meditation. Ally's workout. Jorge's music. Making time for these things was important even before the pandemic. But the challenges brought on by COVID-19 exacerbated what teachers already knew: Teaching is a demanding profession. The media bombards us daily with news of teacher shortages and challenging working conditions. In fact, many parents these days actively dissuade their children from pursuing a teaching career, despite their trust in their local public schools being the highest in decades (Stanford, 2022).

While this is troublesome, we also know plenty of teachers who are thriving. They do so because they have figured out how to deal with that dichotomy. How to make time for the joy and manage the challenge. And you will be one of them. You already have things in your life – outside of teaching – that bring you joy. That's why the approach to healthy living is entirely different for every educator, based on life circumstances, preferences, privileges, and more. And it can change every year, even from month to month.

Consider this book your sandbox, a place to play with ideas, an exploration into what might feel right for you. Teaching can be overwhelming. Going into it with your healthy living plan intact is a good way to insulate yourself from the daily busy-busy and provide you with what you need to be healthy and vibrant in this field. And yes, there were still plenty of days where fear or anxiety won the battle in Katy's day, in Ally's day, in Jorge's day. But when thinking about healthy living, it helps to adopt a both/and approach. You know the old trope about putting your own oxygen mask on before helping others? Exactly.

Real Talk

> Much teacher resilience can be attributed to mindset, and teachers who recognize that they are whole, complete, multitalented, and multifaceted humans – who experience both failure and success in work and home – have a stronger chance of being well in both environments. That "third place," be it a weekly yoga session, weeknight pickleball, Monday afternoon book club or what have you, can provide a time frame that forces teachers to step away from their classroom selves and into joyful experiences that do not revolve around the classroom.
> —Monica McEnerny, Madison Center for Civic Engagement

Why all this talk of healthy living? Well, research tells us that teachers' perceived state of health is strongly associated with their intention to stay in the profession (Casely-Hayford et al., 2022). In other words, **the healthier a teacher feels, the more likely they are to remain in teaching**. It's pretty commonsensical, but feeling healthy matters. And it's not enough to *be* healthy. You actually have to feel it.

We know you can't self-care your way to health and sustainability. Let's take a moment to consider the term "self-care." The extraordinary Audre Lorde, professor, writer, feminist, poet, and civil rights activist, tells us, "Caring for myself is not self-indulgence. It is self-preservation, and that is an act of political warfare (2017, p. 130)." Lorde asserts that caring for one's self is not laziness, self, or self-indulgent; it is essential to maintaining one's self.

> Set your schedule for the week ahead. Designate personal and work time. Hold to it!
> —Tristan Upson, Middle School English Language Arts Teacher

Indeed, teaching is a field where self-preservation is critical. It is a field that will take and take if you let it, especially from people with historically marginalized identities who already have too much of society's history and burdens placed upon them. Self-care as self-preservation takes on a special meaning for educators, who often work in broken systems built on taking,

taking, taking, on a culture of never enough, and on an expectation of sacrificing everything for one's students.

Models of this are everywhere. Consider all of the movies and books where teachers are heralded as heroes, as they sacrifice their health, relationships, and futures. Sadly, these heroes often end up with their personal lives in tatters. And this sacrifice of self is rewarded by messages that permeate culture. Teachers, predominantly women, are part of an economy that has long undervalued care work, has paid women less, and is gendered in terms of who historically moved from teaching to administration. Shame and sacrifice are the tools of a system that uses the mantle of teacher-as-hero to prod teachers into making decisions against their own health and welfare.

Lorde reminds us that when we push against structures and systems that were designed to control and promote (in this case) a teacher-as-hero culture, we are doing resistance work. This doesn't mean shirking the work. On the contrary, it means working hard and being present in your system, working for change and connection, and for your students. But it also means understanding when to say no and scheduling your healthy living practices in a non-negotiable way. It means honoring your daily commitment to a sustainable life despite working within the context of often-broken systems.

Debunk the Myths
Dr. Devon Price tackles some of these issues in her book, *Laziness Does Not Exist* (2021). She describes the following three lies that we think apply well to teaching. The first "lie" is that your worth is your productivity. Whew. This one hits hard. For many of us, this myth is ingrained at a very young age. The economy, of course, thrives on this. So do most professions. But it's especially tricky when the nature of your work is infinite. Student learning is infinite. There's always more you can teach, more you can prepare, more you can assess. The boundary, therefore, has to be drawn by you. We both lived much of our public school teaching life with to-do lists, and we still do. We had to learn the hard way that these to-do lists, complete or not, do not define our worth or our ability to be a good teacher. We were good teachers even if we didn't finish grading those projects that day. When you are falling asleep, do you ever think about the projects or papers you still need to assess? We suggest you also think about the fact that you finally connected with that one student (remember the both/and perspective?). That is a teacher-sustaining behavior. While we all need to be productive, Dr. Price reminds us that we have worth beyond our never ending to-do lists.

Dr. Price's second "lie" is that we can't trust our own feelings. This idea that listening to our own bodies' cues is somehow self-care is also discussed in the podcast, *We Can Do Hard Things*. It's a little nuts, but here we are.

> *That's how divorced we are from our bodies: that we see eating, breathing, walking around, away from the computer, taking time for ourselves or being a participant in our communities as self-care, rather than that's what being a living human being is. That's what we have to do.*
>
> (Doyle, 2023)

We acknowledge that, in teaching, we do need to compartmentalize at times. For example, if our partner said something that upset us right before school, we still need to be present for students. After all, the students show up whether or not we are ready! Listening to yourself is crucial. We need to listen to our feelings and body cues, to trust our own needs, even while teaching. We must allow ourselves to be human, to have needs and to have them fulfilled, in order to do the same for our students. In this system, where it can be hard to find time to even use the bathroom, we often avoid our own internal cues and feelings. This is not a teacher-sustaining behavior.

Dr. Price's third lie is that there's always one more thing you must do. This one is pernicious in teaching. And it's complicated because, well, there is always one more thing you CAN do. Well-meaning coaches, interventionists, principals, and others will point out the many things you could be doing. Of course we need to constantly grow, reflect on our practice, and try many different strategies to meet the needs of our students. But it is hard to make a healthy life if you are always (always!) feeling like you are never enough.

Speaking of never enough, Human Giver Syndrome is "the contagious belief that you have a moral obligation to give every drop of your humanity in support of others, no matter the cost to you – thrives in the patriarchy, the way mold thrives in damp basements" (Nagoski & Nagoski, 2019, p. 99).

Much of society and its many systems tell women they are expected to give their time, attention, affection, and bodies to the needs of other people before their own. These messages promote the idea that women should always be pretty, happy, calm, and constantly attentive to the needs of others (Nagoski, 2019), which can perpetuate emotional exhaustion in teachers (Freudenberger, 1974; Maslach & Jackson, 1981). Since approximately 75% of US teachers are women, issues that affect women disproportionately affect teachers. Regardless of your gender identity, however, we know that emotional exhaustion can lead to burnout. When you combine teaching with caregiving, you have a double whammy of potential human giver syndrome, which takes a big toll on our health.

> **PERMISSION SLIP**
>
> YOU ARE HEREBY GRANTED PERMISSION TO:
> - TAKE A BREAK
> - IGNORE EMAIL WHILE EATING LUNCH
> - USE THE BATHROOM
> - WATCH FUNNY PET VIDEOS
> - CLOSE YOUR EYES

In your healthy living plan, you'll need to fight these myths, lies, and expectations. In doing so, you are doing revolutionary work. You are making teaching a more humane and human-centered field. One that parents will encourage their children to pursue. A mindset of "I am never enough" can quickly become exhausting and debilitating. And it works directly against a sustainable teaching life. Teachers who focus too much on all of the things they *should* be doing will quickly feel that they are not making a positive impact. That's a big problem, because a lack of professional efficacy is a key component of burnout (Maslach, 1978) and a strong predictor of teacher attrition (Alexander et al., 2020). In short, **putting your health first IS putting your students first**. That is another teacher-sustaining behavior. When you feel healthy, and when you feel like you're making a positive difference, you're more likely to stay in the profession.

Lean on Your Community

Most Americans live in a deeply individualistic society. We're told that if we just work hard enough, we will succeed. The current self-help culture is part of this messaging: It's your fault if you are not thriving. You just need to take these supplements, use this app, follow this program (remember the candle and the bath?).

We're the first to admit that hard work is often one ingredient of success. But success is also related to capitalism, colonialism, and a factory model of education, which – to be fair – is another book entirely. We'd like to highlight the role that a community also plays in one's success. Take a look at a couple of historic policy efforts within the US, for example. John F. Kennedy signed the Community Mental Health Act of 1963, establishing community mental health centers across the US for people experiencing mental illness (Substance Abuse and Mental Health Services Administration, 2023). The disability rights movement also emphasized community care, leading to the passage of the Americans with Disabilities Act in 1990, which supported the rights of differently abled people to live in their own communities.

Community care has long been a way of life in many communities across the globe (including in the US), particularly multi-generational communities where the responsibilities of the community are directly tied to the thriving and needs of all individuals. This can be seen in any setting where neighbors are supported in daily living, where a community wraps around members in need. Providing resources, care, guidance, and strong relationships to community members can lead to increased feelings of well-being, safety, belonging, and resilience.

In caring professions like teaching, community care is an essential part of sustainability. Let's look again at what research tells us about teachers who persist. It's clear that social connectedness and support from colleagues are significantly associated with teachers' intention to continue teaching (Thomas et al., 2021). This suggests that, **when we support one another, we're more apt to sustain in this profession**. For new teachers, this is a clarion call to find (or build) your community!

For some folks, finding or building your community can feel like a daunting task. You walk into a new school and system and wonder about your place. It takes energy and intention to reach out to others, especially for those of us who are introverts. First, know that you are not alone. Despite the teacher-as-hero narrative, the whole building (dare we say the whole district?) is there to help you and your students. We'll explore how to build your own community of care throughout this book. One concrete first step, however, is to find an accountability buddy.

We find external accountability to be really helpful when working toward a goal. For example, we both struggled to exercise in the morning. Katy met a friend at 6:30 AM for a little over two years. Even if it was raining or ridiculously cold outside, Katy would think, "I can't let her down!" Similarly, Penny and her teenaged son met at 5:45 AM, using a couch-to-5K app to start their own running habit at their local fitness center. She really (really!) didn't want to wake up that early, but succeeded because she felt she was doing it for him. He probably felt he was doing it for her. Such is the power of accountability buddies.

Who can be your accountability buddy? And what might you need them for? Perhaps they will help you leave at a certain time, stopping by your classroom to say, "Hey! It's time to go. That assignment will be there to grade tomorrow." Or maybe they will meet with you every day for a non-work-related conversation during lunch break. Perhaps it's a walk after school. Whatever it is, enlist your friends and colleagues to help you live more healthily, in a way that works for you.

Make It Through the Tunnel

In their fascinating book, *Burnout: The Secret to Unlocking the Stress Cycle* (2019), the Nagoski sisters explain that, like tunnels, all emotions have beginnings, middles, and ends. To let our emotions and nervous system settle, we must go through the tunnel and get to the other side. Getting stuck in the tunnel can harm our physical and mental health. Teaching is so deeply relational and emotional that each day contains considerable stress. That stress can build up over time and make us sick. How many teachers have made it through the first part of the school year, only to get sick over a holiday? When rest is finally an option, the brunt of the exhaustion and unprocessed stress catches up to us.

Physical activity is the very best way to move through the tunnel of difficult emotions and situations (Nagoski & Nagoski, 2019). That is why we are advocating for daily exercise, which can be a sacred time to move through the tunnel. Other ways, according to Nagoskis, include breathing exercises, positive social interactions, affection, and creative expression. This is why we see so many studies about the importance of mediation to fight stress, the epidemic of loneliness, and the importance of physical touch and creativity.

Guess what? This also applies to students. Consider how you can help them through the tunnel. Big standardized test? Longer recess! Stressful news cycle? A mindfulness activity to start the lesson. Struggling at home? A lunch date with a friend. **Everyone needs a little help through the tunnel**.

Block Out Personal Time

We have all sorts of important appointments blocked out on our calendars. Why don't we schedule our personal time in the same way? Veteran teachers tell us to schedule exercise, friend/family time, and downtime in the same way. It's all too easy to let all the obligations eat up all of your time. That is a quick way to burnout in teaching. Your personal time helps you process, reflect, and stay healthy. Consider how you can block out time for yourself. Is it a recurring meeting on your calendar for a weekly yoga class or a walk with a friend? Schedule it like a doctor's appointment. It really is that important.

Envision the Donut

Each morning Katy listens to meditation teacher Jeff Warren on Calm.com. He guides her through 10–15 minutes of meditation while being just what she needs: funny, accessible, kind, supportive, and not sappy. He uses the metaphor of a filled donut (we can get behind that!) to think about self-care and healthy living. The outside of the donut is the community, systems, and policies; the filling inside is the personal health you can control. While we recognize that the outside impacts our health and well-being and that we must work to improve and change them, we want you – as a new teacher – to think carefully about the inside. Maybe it's exercise, maybe it's eating more healthily, maybe it's getting enough sleep, maybe it's time with loved ones. You know yourself best. What are the things you must do to stay healthy each day even if the outside is crumbling? What's inside your donut?

Make Time for Joy

Unless it fuels you and makes you feel good, Sunday nights should be used for rejuvenation, relaxation, and rest. What does that look like for you? Is it binging a show or watching a movie? A long chat with a friend or family member? Plan on a Sunday evening away from your computer and email. @BishopChemNBCT sums it up nicely:

> *I love zen hobbies. I cricut, have fish aquariums, and just started working with clay. Sunday scaries aren't easy to navigate but when I have something that occupies my mind and body, I focus on now, not Monday. Btw I've taught for 22 years and just figured this out.*

Back to the teachers-as-heroes myth. Teachers are not "saving" students. The narrative that students need to be "saved" breeds a kind of saviorism that isn't helpful. In most cases, it is harmful, especially to students from historically marginalized groups, and it's often based on deficit thinking, foregrounding what the students *don't* have rather than what they do.

And we know that teacher-as-hero or savior is not sustainable for teaching living a healthy life. What if we instead considered different ideas about this: Teacher as Guide, Empowerer, Access Giver, Learning Maximizer, or Resource Provider? They might not be as snazzy as a Hero, but arguably more important.

Sleep and Rest

Scientists are learning more and more about the importance of sleep. Adults need between seven and nine hours of sleep a night to stay healthy. Sleep is where we consolidate memories, rest our bodies, and recover from the day. This is especially important for educators, given teaching is such a high-energy, relational job. Sleep is even referred to as the "invisible workplace" for all of the benefits that it brings us (Nagoski, 2019, p. 166). Getting enough sleep is not selfish, or wasteful; it is essential to your health and well-being in education. To stay healthy, researchers tell us we need to focus on good sleep habits, such as avoiding your phone right before bed and sticking to the same bed time routine as much as possible.

> Everyone benefits from a you that is rested and happy – yourself most of all.
> —Tristan Upson, Middle School English Language Arts Teacher

Many educators have a hard time with this. Our brains are firing all day long, solving problems and managing emotions, learning, and experiences. If you just can't turn that brain off, @HartofLearning suggests you empty your mind of worries and to-dos by writing them down, either in a journal by the bed or on an app like Google Keep, which they like because "… you can access it from any device, share lists with others (delegate to parents helpers when possible)." And then you can turn back to sleep, with your tasks outlined for the next day. Often, this emptying of burdens is what is needed to put the mind at ease.

The busy brain syndrome happens to all of us and can disrupt sleep, especially on a Sunday night. Here are a few ways to deal with that. To ease your mind, @MrKinetik suggests this approach: "Write three things that spark joy that you can do on Monday, a few people you will talk to, and do something you love Sunday." In this way, you might find yourself looking forward to aspects of Monday and sleeping better Sunday nights.

And rest? Take it from Leesa Renee Hall, "Rest isn't a reward for work; it's part of the work (2022)." Rest is imperative for recovery, moving through emotions and stress (which we will talk about next!), but also reflection and reimagining. Teaching is iterative, and because days are full, teachers need time to rest, reflect, and to try again the next day. So forgive yourself if you need to stare into space for a while, lay on the floor after work, or lay on the couch with your cat. Rest is part of the work.

 Dig Deeper

- **Read:** *The Laziness Lie* by Devon Price
- **Listen:** *We Can Do Hard Things Podcast*, episode 303 with Devon Price
- **Read:** *Rewrite the Story You Tell Yourself about Teaching*: https://www.cultofpedagogy.com/unshakeable-angela-watson/
- **Lay down, then read:** *Rest Is Resistance: A Manifesto* by Tricia Hersey

Reflect, Dream, Plan

Reflect on what's inside your donut. Choose one or more of the questions below and free-write your answers:

- What strategies have you tried in the past to support your healthy life?
- Which have worked for you?
- What new approaches do you want to try?
- What support would help you be more successful?
- What might these practices look like in real time?
- How might you fit them in?
- How can you get more rest and sleep?
- Who can be your accountability buddy?

Build Your Playlist

> What song inspires you to take care of yourself?

Identify Your Big Three

From your reflections above, identify three steps toward healthy living. They can be big or small. What approaches to healthy living while teaching will you schedule, hold yourself accountable to, and practice regularly?

1.

2.

3.

2

Managing Time

> **Chapter Overview**
> Time. It seems everyone is short on it, especially teachers. So it's important to head into teaching with a plan for how to make the most of your time. How can you allot precious time for yourself, your health and well-being? This chapter will give you the inspiration, tools, and space to do just that.

Connect

One evening during Katy's first year as a teacher, long past dinner time, she looked outside the windows of her classroom. It was dark. She looked back at her to-do list and saw only a few items left on it. So she stayed and finished them, diligently crossing off items on her list. She drove home, ate a late (and somewhat pathetic) dinner, and went to bed. When she went to school the next day, she made another list. And it was at least ten items longer than the day before. How did that happen?

Katy had yet to learn a key principle in this profession: **The number of tasks a teacher can accomplish will always exceed the amount of time they have to accomplish them.** Period. There was no way she would be able to complete every list, every day, without exhausting herself and ignoring her personal well-being. It took her far too long to realize this, that she needed to accept not getting everything done. Katy came from a "be the first to arrive and the last to leave" kind of family. Completing only *some of the to-dos and setting aside the rest seemed implausible. Yet in teaching, it is totally necessary. This was a hard "both-and" for her to learn.*

This chapter is about just that. How do teachers manage their time and create boundaries around their work so they can feel both productive and rested? Both accomplished and rejuvenated? While this is not an easy task, we hope we can shorten your learning curve.

Real Talk

Take it from these teachers. You don't have to wait years to gain this knowledge. It's here for you now!

> Let go of the expectation that anything in your classroom will go perfectly, and to prioritize your own well-being. If you spend your entire weekend and every night of the week planning you will quickly get burnt out, and it won't matter how good your plans are. You will likely need to do some work outside of the school day, but make sure you structure your non-work time so that you can get the rest and rejuvenation you need to be happy and healthy, and to show up for the kids.
> —Amelia Wurzberg, Literacy Coach

Amelia is on to something here. You'll need to let go of perfection. You don't have to have the most creative layout to your classroom, the perfect bulletin board, the cutest reading area. These things don't happen overnight. Prioritize what's most important: planning for instruction, giving students' feedback, building relationships, and communicating with families. Amelia is right that if you get rest and rejuvenation outside of school you will be able to show up more fully (and positively) for your students, their families, and your colleagues.

> It's ok to not "do it all." It's ok to have boundaries. It's ok to prioritize yourself. It's ok to take your weekends to yourself. You will be a better teacher because of it! And most of all, don't forget to laugh with your kids.
> —Sophie Branson Gill, Assistant Principal

> **PERMISSION SLIP**
>
> YOU ARE HEREBY GRANTED PERMISSION TO:
> - SAY NO TO SERVING ON A COMMITTEE
> - WAIT UNTIL NEXT YEAR TO CHAPERONE THE DANCE
> - ASK FOR 24 HOURS TO CONSIDER A COMMITMENT

Sophie reminds us that it is okay to protect your health and wellness, and that in fact it makes us better teachers. We also appreciate that she reminds us to take time for joy and laughter as an essential way to connect with students and enjoy your work. There will ALWAYS be more to do that you can. Do what is MOST impactful every day. Know it won't feel like enough. Practice being okay with that.

> You cannot be everything to everyone and still take care of yourself. The word no is underused. Don't be afraid to politely decline. You don't need to give a long-winded explanation for why.
> —Middle School Math and Science Teacher

To avoid overload, remember you're still at the start of your professional journey. As a beginning teacher, it's ok to focus on your mentoring meetings, on your department, team, or grade level meetings, on parent meetings, on staff meetings. That's plenty of meetings! When the committee (or other service) invitations come, be ready to think about how you'll integrate them into your other commitments before blurting out, "Sure!" Practice saying things like:

- I really support this idea. Let me review my schedule and capacity to see if I might be able to participate.
- May I have 24 hours to think about it? I'd want to make sure I could fully commit before saying yes."

Need to say no? Try one of these:

- I appreciate your thinking of me, but I'm just not able to add another thing right now.
- Right now my time is all accounted for. Can we revisit this idea next year?

Try to withstand the awkward pause, even the guilt you might feel deep in your heart (or is that just us?). You don't have to do everything. You don't have to be everything. You're a teacher! You're literally shaping the future of our democracy: the next generation of citizens.

> I do not talk about school with my spouse after 6:00 in the evening. I do not use my cell phone for anything school related. I keep social media separate from school and parent relationships. Finally, I do not check email after 4:30 and on weekends.
> —Michael Rapoport, Fifth Grade Teacher

Managing time is tricky. People will tell you to focus on what's most important. But how do you know what that is? This section offers several suggestions and resources. Pick and choose what works best for you. Try the ideas on for size. Kick those that don't fit to the back of your closet like a pair of uncomfortable shoes.

> Perfectionism, the insidious notion that we must not just be good, we must excel at everything we do – classroom management, lesson planning, color-coded classroom supplies, and picture-perfect decor – can be an especially powerful drive among new teachers.
> —Sarah Gosner (2023)

Don't Let Perfect Be the Enemy of Done

This is especially true when lesson planning. It's easy to fall into an hours-long journey into planning for lessons to make them PERFECT. Well, as any experienced teacher will tell you, no lesson goes perfectly. And all those hours of planning will likely be interrupted by… you name it: fire alarm, a meltdown, a last-minute schedule change. So save yourself the frustration. Plan an engaging lesson, with plenty of flexibility, knowing that it might have to change.

It's also helpful to avoid the perfectionist tendency more generally. We've all seen the social media posts. The ones with perfectly colorful organized classrooms, labeled bins, elaborate bulletin boards, gorgeous borders, and color schemes. Every single detail and area is perfectly curated, organized, and thoughtfully designed. And then there is reality. You have the classroom you were given, the supplies that already exist, and, if you're lucky, the supplies you can order each year, and your time. If you aspire to make the space perfect, you will be fighting a losing battle. It's like brushing your teeth while eating Oreos. An active, engaging classroom becomes messy. Learning is messy. And not all schools have the resources to design the optimal learning environment. We aren't suggesting you need to settle for a messy and disorganized classroom. We are suggesting that you do the best you can each day, with the limited time and resources you have. Accepting that it won't be perfect is an important part of this.

All in all, there is no perfect teacher. Some of your peers will have creative displays of student work. Others will have fabulous bulletin boards and laminated games. Still others will have morning meetings that are dynamic and creative. Remember, comparison is the thief of joy. You bring gifts to teaching that are important and uniquely you.

> Understanding the difference between healthy striving and perfectionism is critical to laying down the shield and picking up your life. Research shows that perfectionism hampers success. In fact, it's often the path to depression, anxiety, addiction, and life paralysis.
> —Brené Brown (2010, p. 68)

Prioritize Your Tasks

When she was teaching middle school, Penny used a matrix to help her separate the urgent from the important. With this tool, she could classify her many tasks, and figure out which ones to focus on first. For example, planning for instruction and helping students grow is the critical work of the teacher *and* there's a timeliness to it. It's both urgent and important. Planning lessons, providing feedback to students, and communicating with families and colleagues about time-sensitive issues? Those go first on your list. But it's also fair to say that what goes into these categories is context-specific. They're not going to be the same from day to day, and certainly not from person to person or school to school (Table 2.1).

Katy likes to use three lists for her prioritization: her Must Dos, Can Dos, and Longer-Term Dos. Your Must Dos for the day and week are time-sensitive. Make a list and get them done! The Can Dos for the day and week have a little more flexibility in their timing. The Longer-Term Dos are often worked on when the inspiration strikes (reorganize your reading area? reimagine a unit that has been a bit stale?). For Katy, inspiration for these often strikes in the summer or on a Sunday (often while doing something unrelated to teaching).

Set a Time to Leave

This one can be hard for some people. After all, you have colleagues who want to talk and check in! You have just two more papers to give feedback on.

Table 2.1 Eisenhower Matrix

	URGENT	NOT URGENT
IMPORTANT	**Do it.** Things that align with your goals, and have clear deadlines and conse-quences for not doing them. *Examples:* Instructional design Student feedback Caregiver phone calls	**Schedule it.** Things without a clear deadline that bring you closer to your goals. *Examples:* Professional development Longer-term curricular planning Collaborations with colleagues
NOT IMPORTANT	**Delegate (or automate) it.** Things that need to be done, but don't require your specific skills or full attention. *Examples:* Reminder emails Blog posts Weekly newsletters Administrivia	**Delete it.** Often things that we keep doing without asking why. *Examples:* Reading marketing emails Making instructional materials/bulletin boards visually "perfect"

We know. But you will have those tomorrow, and tomorrow, and tomorrow. Try setting a time by which you will leave each day. Some days you'll encounter a staff meeting that runs late. But try to make it most days. An accountability buddy can help you with this one. Or perhaps you have an afterschool commitment, ideally something that helps your healthy living goals, and you need to make it there on time. That way you can also blame leaving on having a commitment. The commitment is to yourself!

Stop Checking Email

Remember in Chapter 1 when we suggested blocking off downtime? Teaching days are FULL. There are so many decisions. So many emotions. So many people! Giving yourself a few hours of downtime each day may require identifying a time of day when you stop checking email. Seriously, how many times have you gotten an email that sends your nervous system into overdrive right before bed? Something you know you must respond to, but dread or worry about? (we're both raising our hands). Yes, at times we all have to respond to things late in the day. But if something is truly urgent, you'll get a call or text. Trust us, you don't really need to be available via email 24/7. That is a sure path to burnout. Your brain and nervous system need time to settle down, to stop problem solving, and to get some space. There are lots of approaches to this, such as taking the email app off your phone so you aren't tempted to look. One thing is for sure: Protecting at least some of your time outside of school to rest and play is essential to sustaining in this profession.

Streamline Assessment

It's time for the big secret. **You do not need to assess every single piece of student work.** Assessment (both formative and summative) and evaluation are complex topics and they are far too important to do justice to here. But we want you to know that, as you develop your own philosophy and approach to "sitting beside" students, you'll need to develop efficient ways to assess student understanding. We have spent many, many, hours grading papers and giving feedback well into the night. This is not a sustainable practice. While giving feedback is very important for students' learning, coming up with a schedule and practice for when and how to give feedback is important.

Assessment comes from the Latin root assidere, which means "to sit beside." Think of assessment as an opportunity to sit beside students, either literally or figuratively, to glean information about what they know and can do. The basic purpose of assessment is to inform your next steps as an instructor and students' next steps as learners. Does the stack of papers on your desk provide you with the necessary information to do this? How about the lab report? The spelling test? The group project? Some will and some won't.

How will you provide students with regular, meaningful feedback, without writing long comments on thousands of papers? Consider using *entry and exit slips*. Those few minutes at the start and end of class are worth their weight in gold. What have students remembered or assimilated? One quick question (or differentiated questions on the board) can tell you what you need to know. Use Padlet, Poll Everywhere, Edulastic… or go old school and use a pencil and paper. Try *interview assessments*. Meet one-on-one with students while others are working on individual or group tasks. This option has the added benefit of helping students who are better at articulating their comprehension orally. Keep the meetings quick and specific. How about *learning journals?* Rotate when you write in students' learning journals so that you are only responding to two or three each day. Of course, *visuals* work too. Ask students to visually represent their new knowledge. Let those who prefer this medium go free form and provide graphic organizers for those who appreciate more structure.

Remember to Be Human

As this book goes to press, AI is proliferating and causing massive change across industries. Education is no different. AI has the potential to personalize learning and be either helpful or harmful to the learning process. We will leave that to other authors to explore in depth! In the meantime, as you know, we have been focused on *simplifying* what you can. So we encourage you to use generative AI to make your job more sustainable. Consider using AI for clerical and administrative aspects of the job, to start. This might include creating rubrics, checklists, outlines, mailing lists, or different levels of texts or math problems. The key is to use AI for the pieces of the job that don't require deeply relational work. Don't lean on tech so hard that it writes parent emails for you. Those need your personal touch and expertise. But AI might be useful in helping you with a first draft or in offering a list of topics to include. Use your judgment. Would you want emails written by AI about your child? Probably not. Consider when to use it to simplify your teaching life, and then edit and adapt for your own context. And for personal updates and tricky situations, let's all be human, shall we?

Give a Gift to "Future You"

What can you do today that you'll thank yourself for tomorrow? Penny knew that she never had time in the mornings to pack a lunch, and she always regretted it later, when she got hungry. Preparing it the night before was her gift to Future Penny. We turned to social media to crowdsource some ideas from experienced teachers and learned that @lavawitch plans her Mondays with precision, down to the nail polish:

> *I pick my fountain pens inks and my nail polish. And make sure I've got a good audio book for my commute. I get to work an hr before most, so I can relax and check my emails, plan, and do my nails. I'm never walking into chaos Monday morning.*

What can you do to put some slack in the system and get ready for the week? Can you fill your water bottle at home so you don't have to take the time to walk across the school and use the one filling station (this seems small, but take it from a formerly dehydrated person, it is not!). Future You will thank you. Identify the things *you* can do ahead of time.

Leave Your Work on the Downhill Slope

Running *down* a hill, coasting *down* a skateboard ramp, hiking *down* a mountain. It's easier to do almost everything when you're not fighting gravity. At the end of the day, we both like to leave our classroom or office poised for the downhill. We leave ourselves brightly colored sticky notes on our desk of what exactly we need to do when we walk in the next day (make these copies, prep those materials, assess this paper) so we don't have to expend the mental energy climbing up the hill (remembering what we need to do).

@MsJHartmann does a similar kind of prep work on Friday afternoon before leaving. Her advice: "Don't leave work on Friday until your room, materials, and copies walk-in ready to go for the following week. The 30–60 extra minutes in the nearly-empty building mean you can walk in on Monday stress free."

Like Jennifer, @mjacobs324 also follows the pre-planning idea of organizing Monday's lessons on the Friday before. She says: "Plan Mondays on the previous Friday. (You don't need to plan the whole week at once.) Leave explicit notes to yourself on your desk. Set up routine, whatever age, to start the day w/an independent activity."

Whatever your strategy – stickies, online calendar, lesson plan book – point Future You in the right direction. Make it easier for yourself to pick up where you left off the day before. You'll thank yourself tomorrow.

Avoid the Second Arrow

The Buddhist concept of the Second Arrow is a helpful one. Christine Runyan (2021) explores it in the with Krista Tippit. This concept dates back to the times of hunter-gathering. When you get hit with the first arrow, you suffer a big blow, such as pain, suffering, loss, all of which we experience. That arrow is unavoidable and happens to all of us, unfortunately. We feel that deep pain. This can manifest in a smaller (but still impactful) way in teaching. A failed lesson, or student interaction. A missed opportunity. An overreaction or underreaction.

What happens next is up to us, in Buddhist thought. After a failed lesson, it's useful to reflect on what we might do differently next time. But some of us tend to perseverate on the negative. In doing so, we get hit by the second arrow, and get hurt all over again. Therein lies the choice. We can accept the pain/regret from the first arrow, learn, and move on. Or we can fall into a spiral of blame or shame. That tricky second arrow looks like rumination. It's a rough road. And for many of us, it happens late into the night. Remember our first chapter's focus on healthy living?

What if we learned to notice the second arrow, see it coming, and decide not to let it hit us? What if we instead set out to learn from what happened, reflect a bit, make adjustments, and move on? Teaching is too challenging and rewarding to brutalize yourself with the second arrow of judgment, blame, shame, and other emotions that can lead to burnout. What if we approached it like social scientist and author Brené Brown instead? She offered,

> *If you're caught in a shame spiral, there are three things you can start doing today to break the cycle: talking to yourself like you talk to someone you love, reaching out to someone you trust, and telling your story.*
>
> (Brené Brown on Oprah.com, 2013)

All of these can stop that second arrow dead in its tracks.

Create Boundaries

Beyond the boundaries already mentioned for email, your phone, and your hours, think about your other boundaries. What will your weekends look like? If you are like many teachers, you will spend some time on Sundays doing a little preparation. That's okay, but try to make sure it doesn't take up your whole day or night. Set a timer to help you control what you will devote to this prep, then stop! And make sure you are healthy for the week to come.

Other boundaries might include ways to stay positive during the day. This might include certain practices, like a 15-minute time in your classroom during lunch to organize your afternoon. That means you might not spend time chatting with colleagues or eating lunch in the staff room. Or, you might find that doing that really fills you up and connects you to your colleagues. You'll find out what works for you.

Boundaries around waking, sleeping, and free time are important, as we have discussed. But also think about your nervous system. Teachers make thousands of decisions a day. Depending on the grades you teach, you'll also respond to the changing emotions of between 20 and 120 dynamic students AND the emotions of the adults in the building. That is a lot. Consider, what boundaries will support your regulating your nervous system? It might be not debating the private versus public school funding with your uncle on Sunday. Or responding to every single email right away. Think about how you can protect your precious mindset and health, and set boundaries accordingly.

Limit Decisions

Picture it. After a long day of teaching you are standing at the grocery store in front of toothpaste. There are at least 30 choices. You simply cannot decide which one. You've made sooo many decisions already that day, and one more seems impossible. You probably have decision fatigue. This term, coined by social psychologist Roy Baumeister, describes the cognitive and emotional drain that comes from making choices. When the brain becomes overloaded with decisions, it starts to look for shortcuts or stops working altogether.

Teachers make a ton of decisions. Some estimate it as high as 1,500 educational decisions each day! It's little wonder we want you to focus on simplifying life. Make something quick from the pantry. Focus on what really matters at home and at school. And, most importantly, do something that fills your cup so you can begin again tomorrow.

As one way to prepare emotionally and restoratively, @TaraG438499 does some of her school work on Sundays, but intentionally stops at 4 PM and takes care of herself with relaxing and chosen activities. She explains:

> *When I was teaching, I stopped school work at 4 pm on Sunday, done or not. I ate comfort food for dinner and spent the evening enjoying one of my two*

passions – listening to music or watching YouTube videos of my favorite AGT or the Voice shows.

Similarly, @staralixstar42 appreciates the predictability of a treat show saved for Sunday evenings. This brings a relaxing routine, and something she can look forward to each Sunday evening.

I have a TV show that I watch an episode of on Sunday evenings. In the fall, it's usually Great British Baking Show. The rest of the year, it can be whatever. Having that routine helps quiet my mind.

Subtract, Subtract, Subtract

New programs or procedures are often introduced without the time to plan or implement them, assuming that time will come from somewhere, while the amount of recess, lunch duty, before or after school duties remain the same. Similarly, teachers who show leadership potential and good classroom management skills are often the ones saddled with more responsibilities and less time to do them. And we want teachers to lead, in fact, we need them to, but in a sustainable way.

We add and we add and we add, in education. Rarely do we subtract. But it's a fallacy that we will get more productivity if we keep piling more on teachers. This is simply not the case. Didn't we see this in the pandemic? Teachers were learning new technology, working round the clock to connect with students, following all sorts of new procedures for in person instruction, taking on more duties as folks became ill. We saw the result: increased teacher burnout, higher rates of stress and anxiety, and lower teacher retention.

So, let's talk about subtraction. And not just the math operation. In the field of business, organizations that subtract tasks are able to get highly focused on what really matters. Subtraction "sets the stage for innovative work, giving us the space to flop, fuss, discuss, argue about and experiment with seemingly wild ideas that can transform an organization and make employees happier and more industrious" (Matuson, 2022). Those of us in education would definitely benefit from removing things in order to experiment!

We know this is a challenge. For a newer teacher, an even bigger challenge still. But we offer ways to take this business lesson into education. We want you to think about how subtraction might help you be happier and more productive. We know there are many things you can't subtract in your work world. But getting clear and focused about your professional goals for each school year is a great start. As eager as you may be to jump into the many committees, trainings, and professional development opportunities, remember that teaching is a profession of perpetual growth, change, learning, and opportunities to do more. It helps to hone your focus. Is this the year (or few months) you will work on improving engagement and participation in your math instruction and curriculum? Then tailor most of your professional development, reading, and curricular design time around that. This doesn't mean you stop caring about the other areas of instruction and teaching; it just means you will be diving deeper into this area for a time. Choose one or two goals for your professional learning to start.

Committees are another place for thoughtful subtraction. Katy learned this one the hard way. In her first five years of teaching, she worked in a school that had 7:45 AM committee meetings before school started at 8:55 AM. She was on so many committees she came in at that time every day. She knew she had to be at one; she just couldn't remember which. She would see some veteran teachers coming in at about 8:15 and, honestly, she was a little smug. She would think, "I've already been here and in this meeting for a half an hour and here you are, just arriving." But the truth is, they were the ones who had set some professional boundaries. Having committee meetings every single day, along with regular staff and special education meetings, was simply not sustainable. It's arguably not even helpful! When you're involved in too many committees, how can you preview each agenda, participate fully, follow up between meetings, and contribute powerfully?

We know a principal who started at a new school and observed that there were a lot of committees. At a faculty meeting early in the year, she listed every single committee on chart paper. There were dozens. Many were overlapping. Some were unnecessary. Some could be combined with others or put on hold. So that is just what the principal did: suspended, eliminated, consolidated. This kind of subtraction is rare in education. The palpable sense of relief and simplification was real. Folks came in and focused on getting ready for the school day, save for a few committees, based on interest and skill area, and those were efficient and focused. What a change!

Meetings are other places ripe for subtraction. We know. There are a lot of them! The ones where you collaborate with other teachers are usually worth it. The community you are building matters. Yet sometimes there are meetings that do not contribute to your instruction or to student success. Consider combining efforts – where you can. Can that separate meeting actually occur during your team meeting? Or perhaps right before or after a staff meeting you're already attending? Or maybe the meeting could actually be a phone call while you walk or commute. Do what is necessary for you and your students to be successful, and learn to limit the rest!

Find Economies of Scale

This is another useful idea borrowed from business. Economies of scale are cost advantages that companies experience when production becomes efficient. The advantage comes when production increases faster than costs because it spreads the cost of production over more units. In other words, it takes less time to prepare five dinners at one time than to prepare one dinner each day for five days. You gain efficiency from being in the mindset of menu planning, not transitioning from another task, already having your materials out, not waiting for the oven to heat up, not having to put dishes away or find a clean cutting board… you get the picture. Find economies of scale in your home life while you get started on this new career.

- What to wear? Unless you wear a uniform to work, that decision greets us every morning. You can always plan your work outfit ahead of time and set it out the night before. It's one less issue in the morning. But think about economies of scale as your superpower, and bam! Plan all five for the week. Each week, @MsJHartmann does just this. She says: "On Sunday put your 5 days worth of clothes on a hook in your room/bathroom, etc. the less thinking required the faster and easier your mornings are!"
- What to have for dinner? How about prepping multiple dinners on one night? Consider making a big batch of something on Sunday, like chili or lasagna. You can eat it for the first part of the work week as leftovers. Or use a cascading approach: Make black bean soup on a Sunday, use the leftovers for tacos on Monday and enchiladas on Tuesday. In a strong example of pairing a joy with a needed task, @AvashiaNeema makes a playlist of songs that gave her joy that week and listens as she preps meals for the week. We love that!
- How to manage lunch? We know, we know. You think we're going to suggest making a week's worth on Sunday. No. Yuck! Who wants a three-day-old sandwich? Instead, here's an idea we absolutely love. It's creative and contains an element of surprise. Gather up four other fabulous adults from your school to divide and conquer the lunch conundrum by creating a "lunch club." Each person in your club makes *five* of the same lunches (economies of scale!) on *one* day of the week. The rest of the week, you simply enjoy what the others have made and brought for you! (Pro tip: This works with fewer teachers too. Even just getting two or three days out of this idea is a huge time saver.)

Frontload When You Can

Borrowing from the field of project management, frontloading means investing time in planning and preparation at the outset of a project to significantly reduce time needed during later stages. Running a smooth classroom is all about frontloading! Identify how you might streamline your work by investing the time up front for significant time savings later. Email lists, for example, are a great time saver in the long run. It takes some time at the beginning of the year, but we recommend setting up your parent/caregiver email list as soon as possible (thank you, Future Me!). This will require some regular updating, but once it's set up, you can easily email the group at any time by putting the email list in the BCC section. Do the same for your teaching team and any other group you want to have queued up and ready to go.

Making student groups is another place you can invest time early for later time savings. Obviously there are times when you want to be intentional about student groupings, but for those random times, use sites such as Flippety to help you make groups, partners, or any configuration fast. Another time saver is the simple tried-and-true popsicle sticks trick. Write a student

News from (Your Class)

Date

Hello families,

- personal greeting

Curricular Updates:

- write updates about each subject and any general news

Life in Grade 5

- Insert a few pictures here

Thanks for reading,

(email address)

Ask your child about:
- quick but specific ideas about what to ask about..such as read aloud books, recent field trips, projects

Wish List (things that would be VERY helpful for our class)
- an ongoing list of helpful items needed for the classroom (tip, always add snacks!)

Helpful Links
- links to school and district websites, calendars, etc.

Figure 2.1 Newsletter Template.

name on a popsicle stick for every student and place them in a cup near your desk. Then you can make partners or groups quickly and shuffle them around based on who is present and who works well together.

Communication strategies like newsletters are another place to frontload. At the beginning of the year, set up your newsletter template. Teachers typically write updates to families at regular intervals. So, spend some time thinking about how you will do this to save time. Set up a template for your newsletters that you can just fill in quickly. Katy's is below, but you can make your own in Google Docs, on your classroom website/blog, or on your school's digital platform like Google Classroom or Seesaw (Figure 2.1).

Dig Deeper

- **Watch** *The Gifts of Imperfection* webinars by Brene Brown: https://brenebrown.com/tgoi-webinar-series/
- **Listen** to Nedra Discuss Boundaries on *We Can Do Hard Things*: https://momastery.com/blog/we-can-do-hard-things-ep-124/
- **Read** *Set Boundaries, Find Peace: A Guide to Reclaiming Yourself* by Nedra Glover Tawwab
- **Listen** to 7 Ways to Prioritize Teaching Tasks When Everything Seems Urgent on *Truth for Teachers*: https://truthforteachers.com/truth-for-teachers-podcast/7-ways-prioritize-teaching-tasks-everything-seems-urgent/
- **Read** *Do Not Disturb: How I Ditched My Phone and Unbroke My Brain 99 Things To Do Instead of Reaching for your Phone* in the New York Times. https://www.nytimes.com/2019/02/23/business/cell-phone-addiction.html

There are, of course, many more ways to manage your time as a teacher. Please brainstorm other ideas and add them throughout (and let us know, we'd love to hear about them). Use the next section to gain clarity about what might work best for you.

Reflect, Dream, Plan

How will you prioritize your time? Draw or write your ideas below. Consider using apps, a journal, categories such as "must do today" and "could do today" and "save for tomorrow."

- ◆ What time will you try to stop working each day? Draw a watch or clock with that number.
- ◆ When will you stop checking work email each day?
- ◆ How will you aspire to start your days in a way that honors your nervous system and energy?

Build Your Playlist

What song inspires you to set boundaries and prioritize your needs?

How can you help Future You? (Table 2.2)

Table 2.2 Design Your Own Version of the Eisenhower Matrix.

	URGENT	NOT URGENT
IMPORTANT		
NOT IMPORTANT		

Identify Your Big Three

Okay, it's action time. We've considered how to prioritize time. Now it's time to name your Big Three. What are big (or even small) ideas or actions you plan on taking to help manage your time (and wellness!) as a teacher? List, draw, or link below. You got this!

1.

2.

3.

3

Managing Emotions

Chapter Overview
Being aware of your emotions and regulating them as a teacher is key to creating a welcoming and inclusive learning environment. Controlling reactivity and keeping your nervous system running smoothly are important for your – and your students' – success. This chapter will help you understand key concepts of self-regulation and co-regulation, how to identify your triggers, how to best work with them, and how to move through the many emotions that come with teaching. Lastly, this chapter will share practical ideas for how to manage and support emotional well-being in the classroom.

Connect

Katy once worked at an elementary school that held staff meetings before school. The good thing about that timing was that the meeting could never run over time, because the kids were coming! The bad thing was that it sometimes set teachers up to be dysregulated and stressed even before the day began. This was especially true if the agenda included challenging topics that really shouldn't be rushed – such as changes in staffing or procedures, delegation of responsibilities, the introduction of a student's all school behavior plan, report cards, or conferences. These could be stressful meetings, with a rushed sense of urgency, because, well… the kids were coming! Dialogue was often cut short, things were said curtly or not at all, and then it was a sprint walk to use the bathroom and be in your classroom for the first students to arrive. Katy would be out of breath getting to the classroom, her mind full of all of the issues, things said or unsaid, and sometimes negativity from the meeting.

Katy learned that playing upbeat music in the classroom boosted her positivity. This in turn helped her feel ready for students. With music playing in the background, Katy stood (ok, maybe even danced a bit) by the door, ready to greet students. And instead of seeing a stressed-out adult, students' first experience of the school day was a welcoming teacher, smiling and glad to see them. This was an important adjustment. Katy had to make sure she had a few minutes for this each day, even if it meant leaving that meeting a few minutes early. She knew it made her a better, more grounded teacher. It was a simple, yet effective, tweak.

Real Talk

Why Self-Regulation Matters

> Don't take student behavior personally. Remember that behavior requires instruction and skill building just like academics. Tap out when you find emotions are escalating. Be the rock. Take advantage of any professional development opportunities for de-escalation practices. Learn the language of regulation and co-regulation.
>
> —Tim Mulligan, Principal

The teacher's emotions set the temperature in the room. So it's important to have self-regulation strategies in place. Self-regulation is the act of managing thoughts and feelings to enable goal-directed actions, and it includes a variety of behaviors necessary for success in school, relationships, and the workplace (Murray et al., 2015). Each of us develops this skill through time and experience with others. Self-regulation grows by interactions with caregivers, families, teachers, coaches, and supportive others. These skills blossom when students are in predictable and supportive environments that meet their needs.

On good days – which are most days we hope! – things run more or less smoothly at school. Productive classrooms are active and sometimes messy places. They are filled with collaboration, conversation, and hands-on experimentation. And throughout, teachers are managing and facilitating many of these academic and social interactions.

With all of that interpersonal interaction, it's inevitable that even teachers would sometimes find it hard to self-regulate. Remember the idea of making it through the tunnel, which we introduced in Chapter 1? Regulation is "the ability to modify emotions and respond to situations with balance, calm, and control" (Healy, 2023). And self-regulation means that a teacher is able to notice the stress and engage in self-regulation to remain calm, compassionate, and available to help a student. This is not always easy! Teachers need clear ways to self-regulate so they can be healthy AND help their students.

Teachers are human too. It's helpful to analyze how we respond to varied circumstances and to identify our triggers, behaviors, and responses. For instance, do certain types of interactions with colleagues seem to affect us more than others? Are there times of day when we exhibit more patience with students? During the more challenging times, it's especially useful to notice what you are feeling. You can even acknowledge it or give it a name. "Hello, stress. I see you." Notice what is happening in your body. Is your breathing shallow? Does your chest feel tight? Identify something you can do about it, in the moment. This may be a minor but intentional shift. For example, close your eyes and deepen your breathing if it's shallow. Get up and move if you're sitting. Sit down for a moment if you're standing. Move your eyes to something out the window. Interrupt the feeling and its hold on you. Then, when you have a longer period of time, find a more private space to self-regulate. Move through and manage the feeling without acting on impulse or reacting negatively. Close the door, metaphorically AND literally. Close your classroom door, the bathroom stall door, the car door, the closet door! Do what it takes to find personal space. Perhaps repeat a mantra to yourself (I can do hard things; I am strong and resilient). Moving through your emotions instead of letting them sit and fester will help you be ready for your students.

PERMISSION SLIP

YOU ARE HEREBY GRANTED PERMISSION TO:
- INHALE
- EXHALE
- PAUSE UNTIL YOU FEEL CALM AND CENTERED
- FIND A QUIET PLACE TO MOVE THROUGH EMOTIONS

> Between stimulus and response, there is a space. And in that space lies our power to choose. And in our choice lies our growth and our freedom.
> —Often attributed to Victor Frankl (Schorling, 2024)

You know those reactions that seem practically automatic? Perhaps you have a sibling who knows exactly what buttons to push? An important key to self-regulation is to move from *reacting* to *responding*. To do so, you need to identify your triggers (the stimulus), pause and avoid reactivity (the space), and select a behavior that helps you attain your goal (the response).

> Check your knee-jerk responses. Take a breath, ask yourself why the behavior you are seeing might be happening and what it brings up for you. Ask yourself what you need to be the mature human you are.
> —Amelia Wurzberg, Literacy Coach

Here's an example. Let's say Penny is teaching English Language Arts. It's the last period of the day, she didn't sleep well the night before, and she's had a headache all afternoon. Her students have been instructed to look for textual evidence in short stories to support their answers to evaluative questions. Kyle, an eighth grader, simply will not stop talking to his tablemates about his plan to play League of Legends after school (the stimulus).

She gently and quietly redirects him several times to get him back on task, and he disregards her each time. She hates when students lose valuable learning time and she also feels disrespected by students who don't respond to her gentle redirection. These two things are definitely triggers for her. Penny is always keen to avoid a power struggle but today she feels particularly short-fused.

An unhelpful (yet understandable) REACTION: Sighing with exasperation, Penny raises her voice and calls out the student in front of others. Kyle, responding to her negative tone and to public censure, refuses to lose face. The situation escalates, resulting in distraction and lost learning time for the whole class and further stress for Penny.

A productive RESPONSE: Penny takes a deep breath and reminds herself that Kyle is 14 and that she's the adult in the room (the pause). She mentally ticks through other options available to her: make a joke, invite everyone to take a stretch break, convert the task into a whole-class activity, change up the groupings via a jigsaw. She quickly uses her knowledge of this student to select the one that she believes will work best in this context (the response).

Consider how you react in various circumstances during your school day. Once you identify your emotional triggers, you can recognize them when they arise, create a mental list of tactics, and be proactive about managing your responses!

Other moves that help with self-regulation (this is the tip of the iceberg, lots of other research, strategies, and ideas exist!):

- Take a physical break (even ten squats by your desk, touching your toes, a walk to the bathroom down the hall) (Healy, 2023).
- Can't leave the classroom? Focus on a LONG exhale, like 4–7–8 breathing. Inhale for 4 seconds, hold for 7 seconds, exhale for 8 seconds.
- Focus on something in the distance, such as a piece of art or a photo (or picture a calm place in your mind). Visit for a few moments and breathe.
- Engage with a fidget, or take a sip of (hopefully still hot) tea or coffee. Pause.

People in the caring professions, such as teachers, social workers, and health care professionals, sometimes experience compassion fatigue. This is "the physical, emotional, and psychological impact of helping others – often through experiences of stress or trauma" (WebMD, 2022). If you care (and we know that you do because you're a teacher!), you will read your students' emotions, listen to their issues, problem solve, and try to help them all day, every day. This can get tiring! Especially if things in the world or local community feel uncertain or worrisome. You might find yourself with very little to give emotionally at the end of the day. That is when to REST (more on this later) and move through your emotions to process and get through the tunnel. For now, know that this is normal, even expected. As you read, you will build a set of tools to manage this condition, to lessen its impact, and to help you thrive in this profession.

> Breathe. Remember that this is a hard job, but you are the adult in the room and what you model sets a tone. Find a friend, get some fresh air, and this too shall pass.
> —Heidi Ringer, Librarian and Former Fifth and Sixth Grade Teacher

Co-regulation Is Key

Now let's talk about co-regulation. Co-regulation is just like it sounds, a process that supports students' development of self-regulation in relationship with caring adults. It's more or less the process of harmonizing with another nervous system!

> *If you are in a room with another person, your brain and your nervous system are reading the state of that person, taking in many cues about how calm or stressed they are. We do this through facial expressions, body language, and even respiratory rate.*
>
> (OTFC, n.d.)

As we mentioned earlier, **teachers set the temperature in the room**. Students feed off of the mood, affect, and attitude of the teacher. The students sense when you are stressed or anxious and it is very much contagious. On the other hand, if you're relaxed and comfortable, students are more likely to be as well.

Luckily, we can co-regulate in our classrooms to help create the kind of environment we want, one that is safe, predictable, and full of trusting relationships. Remember that students need to make it through the tunnel too, and studies show that our internal states are "profoundly contagious" (Nagoski & Nagoski, 2019, p. 136). According to current research, sharing a physical space with someone (in our case, a classroom) in some cases actually synchronizes heartbeats. When experiencing something together (an emotional scene in a read aloud book, for example) students' emotional responses can synchronize. Students begin to align their facial expressions, movements, and vocal patterns with others (Cacioppo et al., 2014). Simply knowing this can help us consider our own impact, and work on collectively co-regulating the classroom in intentional ways.

While co-regulation may feel daunting, you don't need to be serene or devoid of any strong emotions. Rather, there are moves you can make to help you co-regulate with students in a positive way. First, focus on creating trusting relationships. Consider the many small moves you make to help students feel seen. We'll bet you don't even think about some of them, but they really add up. Looking up and at students as they enter, welcoming them by name, asking about the game or the show or the new song. Each of these subtle connections sends the message that "you matter." These actions help students feel safe and regulated. They are reinforced by larger and more formal actions, such as advisory or morning circle, anywhere positive social relationships can be cultivated and modeled. In these spaces, students learn from and connect with each other, and feel seen and heard.

In addition to building relationships, provide structure and flexibility. Practices like morning meetings and advisory help students feel a sense of security in structure. Predictability is helpful for many students. Writing the schedule on the board helps those students who are feeling hypervigilant or anxious understand and plan for a predictable schedule. This doesn't mean you can't be spontaneous; it just means that students know what to expect each day. At the same time, flexibility helps students who feel dysregulated. Can they do their assignment in flexible seating? Soft starts, such as reading or drawing independently, are a gentle and choice-based way to help students bridge that gap between home experiences and school. Flexible choices help students feel more in control and, therefore, more able to self-regulate.

> There is no courage without vulnerability. Courage requires the willingness to lean into uncertainty, risk, and emotional exposure.
> —Brené Brown (2012)

Co-regulation is also the result of a classroom community that feels safe. Students need to know that it's ok to talk about emotions. Social emotional learning programs, such as those based on Collaborative for Academic, Social, and Emotional Learning (CASEL, 2023) standards, help students learn how to self-regulate. Such learning can also be embedded throughout the day, connecting dialogue about feelings to whatever the class is reading. When talking about emotions becomes the norm, students acquire permission and language that helps them express when they feel scared, anxious, or frustrated. They can also learn how to pause and work through the feeling, so it doesn't overwhelm. This might look like regular morning meetings with a theme, such as a "State of the Class" (modeled after the State of the Union presidential speech) where students discuss what is going well and what needs to be improved in the class. It can also include a "What's Up in the World" where students find out the facts about what is happening in the world and discuss how they are feeling about it.

> Our nervous system calms down when we feel tended to.
> —Christine Runyan (2021)

Tools for Co-regulation

Remember the music example from the beginning of this chapter? Katy regularly used music to regulate her own nervous system after tense staff meetings, and this self-regulation carried over into co-regulation. This was no accident! Music can have profound impacts on our nervous systems. Much of this can be intuitive, and you probably already do this in your personal life (listening to upbeat music to get going on your day, relaxing music at night to get ready for sleep), but the same applies and can be extended to the classroom. Do students need to calm down after recess? Play slower music (35–50 beats per minute). Need to energize a tired class? Play more upbeat music (100–160 beats per minute) (Healy, 2023). Spotify has playlists in all of these ranges (preview first for NSFW issues!). Music is a powerful co-regulation tool.

During the COVID-19 pandemic, students needed a safe, calm, and relaxing environment after recess or a disruption in routine. Many of Katy's students found this in art activities that included personal drawing, mindful mandala coloring, or other paper crafts such as origami. These activities let her students' nervous systems regulate, while giving Katy a chance of a pause as well. Movement breaks are also a key feature of a co-regulated class. Students can't sit for long! Stretch breaks, group yoga moves, silly song/dances, Go Noodle activities, are all co-regulation strategies that also promote engagement and learning (yay, neuroscience!). So schedule these breaks into your lessons, and be confident that you are helping with co-regulation AND learning.

There are also ways to weave regulation into the classroom environment. You'll see these often in classrooms that feel homey, inclusive, and responsive to student behavior, mental health, and wellness. Calm corners are intentionally designed spaces in the classroom that are oriented toward calming an overstimulated or overactivated nervous system. You'll see these called peace corners, quiet spaces, or other names. Invite your students to help you design and name your own. They may contain a bean bag chair, some fidgets, coloring pages, and perhaps noise canceling headphones. Students can self-select to visit this space at any time for brief periods to regulate. This should not be a punishment or time out space, or a place to escape instruction, but a space available to all students at any time. Like any shared space, this needs to be taught and modeled to students, and to all support staff who work with students, so it can be used by students comfortably (Healy, 2023).

Often, student dysregulation is from a lack of their basic needs being met. They might be dehydrated, hungry, or tired. Do not underestimate the power of a well-stocked snack closet or shelf. This could be located in the calm corner or somewhere else. Parents, caregivers, and your budget can help you stock it with high-protein snacks such as energy bars and snack mixes. Having these snacks available promotes learning and wellness and even helps prevent depression and anxiety (Healy, 2023). Snacks for the win!

We also invite you to think about your personal calm corner in the school. For Katy, no joke, it was a supply closet. It was mostly quiet, and it was there that she could meditate, listen to music, or connect with a loved one during the day. She kept the lights off and took 15 minutes during lunch to regroup. Where might your calm corner be, even just for a few moments in the school day?

One thoughtful, trauma-informed approach we like that normalizes having big emotions and self-regulation is creating calm kits with students. These are personal creations and can be as simple as a small bag with self-regulation tools selected by the student. Consider creating these early in the year with your students. Students select items that help them personally to relax. Teachers can supply some of the materials and they can be donated or supplied by a Parent Teacher Organization (PTO). These can include pipe cleaners, fidgets, small toys, coloring pages, art supplies, and special pens. Of course, the use of these needs to be normalized and modeled so students learn how to use them without distracting others, and engaging with learning activities as they can.

Of course, think about a personal calm kit for yourself. What would it include? A journal, some tea bags, a favorite picture, or item? You can create one too – you deserve these things too.

Dig Deeper

- **Read** *How to Teach Self-Regulation* (Edutopia): https://www.edutopia.org/article/how-teach-self-regulation/
- **Review** *What Is Emotional Regulation (and tips for teaching it)* (We Are Teachers): https://www.weareteachers.com/emotional-regulation/
- **Listen** *On Being Podcast: On Healing Our Distressed Nervous Systems*: https://onbeing.org/programs/christine-runyan-on-healing-our-distressed-nervous-systems
- **Read** *Regulation and Co-Regulation: Accessible Neuroscience and Connection Strategies that Bring Calm into the Classroom* by Ginger Healy.
- **Watch** *The Art of Co-regulation*, Rabia Ahmed, Tedx Talks: https://www.youtube.com/watch?v=XFJir3Tg-W4

 **Reflect, Dream, Plan**

How do you react when…

- students don't do what you ask them to?
- students don't listen to you?
- students become loud or unfocused?
- your lesson goes sideways?
- a colleague drops a ball?
- a teammate is repeatedly late to meetings?
- a student's caregiver doesn't show up for a meeting?

Notice any triggers? Record them here:

Remember to S.T.O.P.

Stop what you're doing.

Take a deep breath.

Observe the present moment. Notice what you're thinking and feeling and identify the various responses you have to choose from.

Proceed. Select the response that helps you attain your goal.

At School
- Use the Calm or Headspace App
- Go for a Walk
- Talk with a Friend
- Draw/Sketch/Color
- Play Music
- Recite Affirmations

At Home
- Spend Time with Family
- Exercise
- Practice Yoga
- Take a Relaxing Bath
- Read
- Go to Bed Early
- Hang Out with a Pet (Borrow One if You Need To!)

You talk about, also, symptoms of this stress on our nervous system that I think I recognize in myself, and we all recognize as being more impulsive, moody, rigid in our thinking, irritable, lashing out, our frustration tolerance; and you could almost see that play itself out in our political life.

—Brené Brown, *Unlocking Us*

Build Your Playlist

Remember how Katy played music to start her day?
How will you feed your nervous system with positive energy?
What's *your* walk-on song? Your psych tune?

Draw your ideal, co-regulated classroom. What are students doing? What are you doing?

Identify Your Big Three

Now it is the time to plan it. What three action steps will you take based on this model to create emotional regulation in yourself and your students?

1.

2.

3.

4

Collaboration with Your School Community

> **Chapter Overview**
>
> It takes a village to raise (and teach) a child. And yet our society is more isolated than ever before. Your school community is key to your success and feelings of efficacy. This chapter will describe the importance of working with others and the ways this can be supportive, improve your teaching, and help you feel good. In it, we will walk you through how to collaborate in your school community in different ways and with different people. We know that you can't do this job alone. Remember, there is a whole system designed to support you.

Connect

It was peak pandemic when Katy's elementary school opened up for smaller groups of students on alternate days. Everything felt tenuous, fragile. Protocols changed every day, and cases came and went in various grades. It's safe to say all teachers were worried, anxious, and trying their best to help students through this challenging time.

Katy's grade level team met almost every day. They discussed curriculum, and shared resources, ideas, and lessons. They discussed students and conferred about how best to handle different situations. When one of them had a childcare issue, or a phone call to take, or an appointment to make, they covered for each other.

They kept the continuity going. But, most importantly, they met as humans. They connected about their families and their lives. They knew what was happening with each other, and this felt more supportive than anything during such an unstable time.

There is great comfort, especially in times of rapid change, in having such durable, consistent colleagues. They serve as a safety net, a sounding board, and a brain trust that tackles the many intricacies and challenges of teaching. They have your back, challenge your thinking, and help you grow in many ways. They also listen to you and let you challenge existing practices, without resistance or negativity.

Real Talk

> Find ONE person who thinks about students and curriculum in a way that resonates with you. If it's someone who has been at the school longer than you, what approaches have worked for them in terms of this school's systems? If you have similar goals, can you divide up a task? For example, one school installed a permanent set of posts for a story walk. Each teacher took charge of creating the pages…and then they had enough for a whole year's worth of walks, and the start of a story walk library for the future. They planned for the present, but would benefit for years. I also found it really useful to ask other teachers' perspectives on approaches with children I found challenging or those who needed a challenge (sometimes the same kid :-)). I would get in a rut, and they would help me think outside of my "go to" approaches.
> —Valerie Bang-Jensen, Professor of Education Emerita

PERMISSION SLIP

YOU ARE HEREBY GRANTED PERMISSION TO:
- NOT GO IT ALONE
- ASK FOR HELP
- BORROW IDEAS
- COLLABORATE WITH OTHERS

The research is in on this one. Teacher collaboration supports both teacher sustainability and student achievement. We know from numerous studies that teacher collaboration combats many aspects of teacher burnout – emotional exhaustion, cynicism/depersonalization, and a lack of professional efficacy (Freudenberger, 1974; Maslach & Jackson, 1981).

A key message of this chapter? **Don't go it alone.** This job is too big for any one person. The media will sell you on a teacher-as-hero trope, where teachers sacrifice everything to save the students! The sage on the stage delivers incredibly moving lectures, and then alone figures out how to reach the most challenging of students, all the while sacrificing their personal lives. This trope is damaging in many ways, as we have addressed earlier, but one of them is surely that it conveys this is a one-person job. This could not be farther from the truth. Sure, the person with the most contact time with students is the classroom teacher. But this happens within an ecosystem where everyone in that building (and hopefully beyond) is there to support and help students be successful.

> Collaboration is one of the most rewarding parts of teaching. If you're lucky to walk into a team that is already collaborative, congratulations! But, if you don't, make a "team" for yourself. Find the teachers who sit toward the front at inservice and nod and ask probing questions, take advantage of opportunities for coaching (and pay attention to the veteran teachers who do too), notice who is helping out on spirit days – those are the ones to seek out to collaborate with. Gravitate toward those teachers – they are the ones who are hungry to collaborate – who love to learn from others and are happy to have to let others learn from them. Surround yourself with those who always want to learn more or try something new, because you'll continue to build each other up each day.
> —Tristan Upson, Middle School English Language Arts Teacher

Tristan's advice to "make a team for yourself" is wise indeed. There is no way (and no need) to be an expert on everything. Let's take a look at both formal and informal opportunities for collaborating and learning from others in schools.

Welcome the Expertise of Others

> It would be impossible to be an expert from the start (even though the pressure they feel is that they should know everything). Rely on experienced teachers in the building for advice and ideas when things feel overwhelming or they aren't sure of the best way to do something.
> —Davida DeLena, Math Interventionist

Schools are filled with specialists and others with deep expertise. As generalists, most elementary classroom teachers must be knowledgeable about a wide range of things and that can feel overwhelming. But the need for others' expertise isn't specific to a grade level or range. Relying on people in the building who have knowledge or experience that can help you and your students doesn't mean you are failing. On the contrary, that's what they are there for! **Adopt an open door and open mind for collaboration.** Coaches, interventionists, bilingual or multilingual specialists, social workers, special educators, guidance counselors, they are all there to support you and your students. (If they are not, they should be somewhere else!)

While meeting with these colleagues can take time, it is usually time well spent. If you bring your work, your ideas, your plans, and a bit of vulnerability to these meetings, these folks will help you improve your instruction, help with particular problems and student needs, and help develop plans for student success. Ideally, you'll meet with some of them weekly. If the meetings don't feel productive, work first on building openness and trust. Then, craft a collaborative agenda to prioritize what needs to get done. Examples of this kind of collaboration include developing instructional materials for small groups; creating behavioral plans and systems for students; focusing on increased reading engagement; and working with families to communicate.

Rely on Your Teaching Team

Your grade level or grade band team, interdisciplinary team, or department can also be a supportive place to look for collaboration. This group typically knows your grade level, your schedule, the challenges you face, and the curriculum. They can help plan events, troubleshoot student and family issues, and break tasks into smaller chunks for each person on the team to do. It is important to develop a strong bond and community with these folks. While not all teaching teams are collaborative, it's good to make every effort to join that community, especially at the start. This will take some time but can yield significant results. And sometimes these meetings can feel stressful. That's why teams like this often benefit from having clear norms. If they don't already exist, you might ask about developing some. Sometimes norms can feel a little awkward or hollow at first. Many of us have been in meetings where we look at norms at the start of the time. Yes, we will hold space for disagreement. We all nod. Yes, we will speak our truths. But when we need the norms, they become essential tools to productive collaboration. They can be simple things, such as "we will start on time, finish on time, focus on solutions, and listen to all voices." They are important guardrails for team meetings as the group can always circle back to these if (when, more likely) things go a bit sideways.

Similarly, assigning roles each meeting can help distribute work more evenly and prevent resentment from building up. Common ones include a timekeeper, note taker, and facilitator, though they do vary. Team meetings can't be a place where the same person takes notes each time "because they are good at it." Newsflash: They aren't. They're just more willing, and they know someone has to do it. Allow a bit of time to reflect on these as the meeting is wrapping up. This is hard to save time for, but so helpful. It takes courage to say, "I noticed we were interrupting each other a bit today" or "I've been taking notes for every meeting," but over time this helps build an honest and trusting community. Having norms and roles you can rely on helps a team run smoothly.

> Positive and intentional relationships with colleagues and administrators are linked with higher job satisfaction and retention among new teachers who are more likely to stay in the profession when they feel a sense of voice, partnership, and inclusion in their schools.
>
> —ASCD, 2024

Find Your Mentors

If you are new to teaching, or more experienced but new to a school, a mentor is super helpful. Hopefully you have been assigned one. Mentors will get you up to speed on the school culture and practices, can help explain the teacher observation and evaluation process, and know where everything is. Katy was a 17-year teaching veteran when she moved to a new school in the middle of the COVID-19 pandemic. She was assigned a fabulous teacher who had been teaching for seven years at that point. Her support and guidance were incredibly helpful. Not only did she help Katy learn the ins and outs of a new district and school quickly, she was able to answer all of her questions and troubleshoot unexpected situations. Do not underestimate the power of this relationship. Everyone new to a school needs a mentor. Keep a list of questions for these meetings and attend every one. Even if you simply go for a walk and talk about the day, it is an important and generative relationship!

If you've not been assigned a formal mentor (and even if you have), your school building is filled with informal mentors. The teacher across the hall, the guidance counselor who stops by, the school chef, these folks are all helpful. You can run ideas or problems by them, get their take on a situation, or simply chat. Informal mentors, especially those who have been at the school for longer than you have, can give you some pointers for how to operate in that particular system. These relationships are important. And if a formal mentor hasn't been appointed, don't be shy about asking one of these wonderful people to be your mentor.

> Find your people…people who are approachable and encouraging, who make you laugh, will share ideas, and will challenge you.
>
> —Julie Smart, Special Educator

Find Your People

Beyond the expertise of specialists and mentors (who are critically important), it is similarly important to find people at school who support you, fill your bucket, offer ideas, listen deeply, and maybe, most importantly, laugh with you. Because, yes, this job can be ridiculous. Kids say and do the most random things. We can honestly say not one single day of this job will be boring. You are constantly facing new and different situations. It helps to have someone (or a few folks) you can share with, who you can trust, who can laugh or commiserate with (but not too, too much, which we will discuss later) daily. It's also helpful, after time and trust builds, to find people who can challenge you in positive ways.

> Build relationships with folks across the school, not just in your teaching team or position.
>
> —Sharon Spector, Guidance Counselor

These might not be the people you would expect. Often finding your people happens organically. It might be a group of new-ish teachers. Or it might be the group that likes to walk during lunch. It could be the person across the hall who touches base with you briefly each day (and just by proximity the relationship begins). No matter who or how or what, who is it that makes you feel good? Seen? Supported? The person who notices when you are not there, who can help find a sub or solve a problem. Or who will send you silly texts and GIFS about teaching. The relationship might not extend beyond school, and that's okay. This kind of work person will make your teaching life infinitely better and is not a formalized role. Seek these out, build these over time.

> Find a mentor or an ally on staff to help you the first year. Get to know important people like office staff, custodians, and paras. Build relationships!
>
> —Amy Whitlock, Middle School Health Educator

Pay particularly close attention to the glue of the school: the administrative assistants, custodial staff, and other hardworking folks who hold the school together. They are consummate problem solvers. Get to know these folks by name. Ask about their families and their favorite activities. Listen. Drop off treats. Not only are they interesting individuals in their own right, they are also the folks who will find you a guest teacher, the ones who will clean up unpleasant things in your classroom, the ones who will find cover for you when you have to run out of the classroom unexpectedly. Build good relationships wherever you can. They won't all work out, but most will and they will be important to you and your health in the building.

Build Your Online Network

What a time to be alive. We have infinite amounts of information available to us. This is both thrilling and completely overwhelming. If you're into social media, you may already have a good handle on this. If not, know that you can build and leverage your online network to support you as a teacher. There are countless educators across the globe engaged in the kind of work you are doing, with different perspectives, strengths, ideas and resources.

Consider using social media professionally as a tool to connect and build your community. We suggest designating at least one platform as a *solely* professional space. Choose a place for you to present yourself professionally and build a community of similar professionals working in education. It can help you build a strong educator network, provide you with realistic views on existing opportunities, and give you insight into a pathway for yourself. Once you select one as your professional platform, don't post here about your holiday in Scotland or about your new nephew, no matter how cute he is. *Do* post about recent professional development that made you think differently, new things you're trying, and readings that inspire you. Use the account to build your educator community and to grow opportunities for yourself. While you do, remember our caution about around "perfect" classrooms and the like. Life is heavily curated online and social media is full of unattainable goals. If it feels healthy, you can use it as a place for inspiration. But we don't want you getting stuck in feelings of comparison and "not good enough." Teacher TikTok and Instagram can be inspiring places, but they can also drain your time and energy. So keep this in mind as you engage in this kind of curation.

Consider too the limitations of where you physically live and work. Help to expand your community, along with the resources and perspectives you share with your students, by learning from others in different geopolitical contexts. You can curate learning for yourself in lots of areas, history, politics, natural resources, the arts… you name it! There are many ways to build collaboration beyond the walls of your school. Do what sustains you, inspires you, broadens your perspective and builds a network for your future.

Dig Deeper

- **Read or Listen** *The Team Check Up: 10 Principles for Building a More Efficient, Effective Teaching Team*: https://truthforteachers.com/10-principles-for-building-a-more-efficient-teaching-team/
- **Review** *Building Teacher Collaboration School Wide*: https://www.amle.org/building-teacher-collaboration-school-wide/
- **Read** *Setting Up Meetings to Empower Teachers*: https://www.edutopia.org/article/leading-effective-meetings-teachers/
- **Review** *Finding Mentoring as a New Teacher*: https://www.edutopia.org/article/finding-mentor-first-year-teacher/

Reflect, Dream, Plan

Keep a running list of questions you have for your formal or informal mentor. Start it here:

Build Your Playlist

Is there a song you like that celebrates people working together? Or one that puts you in the mood to partner with others?

Identify Your Big Three

From the ideas above, select three action steps or ideas that can help support collaboration this year!

1.

2.

3.

5

Building Meaningful Curriculum

> **Chapter Overview**
> This chapter is here to demonstrate that creating meaningful curriculum with your students can also help *you* maintain a sense of purpose and satisfaction. You'll get a broad overview of how to do this, as we describe a few powerful pedagogies. And then of course we'll offer additional resources for you to explore, and a set of actions and ideas for your toolkit. Let's go!

Connect

Meaningful curriculum is often rooted in what students care about. As a teacher, Katy learned quickly to connect the curriculum to students' interests. She understood that motivation was key to engagement, and learning what motivates students was essential to helping them learn. And when her students found meaning, purpose, and engagement, the energy spread to Katy and fueled her day-to-day work.

Alan was a fifth grader in Katy's class. In teaching how to write persuasive essays, Katy introduced the genre with topics accessible to many young adolescents, such as the removal of chocolate milk from the school lunch, shortened recess, or the requirement of school uniforms. Now, Alan wasn't at all interested in chocolate milk, in school uniforms, or in recess for that matter. But he was very interested in geography.

He poured over maps. He played games on the computer naming countries, rivers, capitals, mountain ranges. He was eager to learn all he could about the world around him. At this time, Russia had just attacked Ukraine and Alan really wanted to understand it. He undertook a huge project, learning about the history of the two countries and their economic and social drivers, in order to write a compelling persuasive essay calling for peace. When he finished, Alan presented this to his class, along with a strong lesson in geography and geopolitics. It was almost a college lecture or class. Katy was astounded. Gobsmacked. She sent the letter to the United Nations as an additional audience. He received a formal letter of recognition back. His voice was heard.

Jonah was a sixth grader in Katy's science class. The fifth and sixth grade science classes were undertaking a big project-based learning (PBL) unit to learn about the watershed around the school. Jonah, however, was pretty sure school wasn't for him. He was much more interested in what his father was teaching him: how to drive the tractor, plow snow, hunt, and tap a sugarbush to make maple syrup. Jonah didn't think he needed what school was selling. Keen to honor student choice, Katy encouraged each group to identify a question they cared about. Jonah's group posed the question, did wolves ever live in Vermont? So their project began. These students interviewed their uncles and grandparents, consulted with the Rod and Gun Club and Vermont Fish and Wildlife, and spoke with other groups to find oral histories and details about the wolf's historical habitat. Their learning culminated by writing an original play to communicate the history of the wolf in Vermont. They performed it on a hillside, complete with cardboard wolves, for the whole school. Jonah couldn't believe that this was school. That he and his friends could talk about hunting and share their learning in a way of their choosing.

This is what school can be, and it can engage both students like Alan, who loved school, and Jonah, who had little use for it. Everyone benefits from meaningful curriculum. Not the least of all the teacher, who gains a sense of purpose from watching her learners connect, develop new skills and knowledge, and increase their affiliation with school.

Real Talk

What does it mean to live a purpose-driven life? If you have gotten into teaching, we can imagine you're already well down the road on this one. Teaching is one of the best ways to connect to meaning and purpose every single day. You are helping people, some of the most vulnerable in society, and everything you do can create more access, inspiration, and interest in a healthy, happy, engaged future. You are dedicating your professional life to a cause bigger than yourself. It is heady, big work.

If you're a teacher, the truth is that most days you can let your head hit the pillow knowing you gave it your very best. You made a young person feel seen, feel safe. You may have inspired them to read a book, to create art, to solve a problem, or pursue an interest. That feeling, that awareness of the work you are doing, can be motivating and fulfilling.

On the other hand, if you feel uninspired, or you're not tapping into that feeling of purpose, you may want to look at your curriculum. Research tells us that **the more teachers feel empowered to make decisions about curriculum and instruction, the more likely they are to remain in the profession**. "Teachers' perceptions of their sense of autonomy and job control, in terms of exerting decision authority with regards to curriculum, student discipline and instruction, was strongly associated with their intentions to remain in the profession" (Casely-Hayford et al., 2022). In a world of worksheets and all-too-shallow activities, it is time for non-disposable work: work that inspires, that connects, that opens doors and provides relevance, agency, real-world skills, and value. This chapter can help you, like Katy, Alan, and Jonah, find that deeper sense of purpose.

> Curriculum should help students see the big picture, make connections, and apply their learning in meaningful ways.
> —Chris Edmin (2021)

Consider this section a delightful appetizer spread on our long, welcoming dining table. There are many savory treats here to sample. They will taste good (lead to you feeling good with high student engagement) and they are just a small sample! These approaches deserve more attention (entire books, actually, so be sure to check out the resources sections). But these appetizers are meant to whet your appetite for teaching and learning that is engaging, exciting, relevant, and purposeful for students AND for you. Let them insulate you from worksheet-itus.

We know you're busy. So look over these conceptual appetizers. We've spread out before you five approaches that have great potential for deep engagement: PBL, service learning, personalized learning, place-based learning, and maker education. We've laid them out separately in this chapter as a way to describe their individual characteristics, but you'll notice that there's plenty of overlap between and among these approaches. Sample a few. See what sparks your interest. Later you can use resources to go deeper and identify the elements that inspire you and fit with your context and students.

> **PERMISSION SLIP**
>
> YOU ARE HEREBY GRANTED PERMISSION TO:
> - START SMALL
> - SAMPLE PROJECT-BASED LEARNING
> - TASTE-TEST SERVICE LEARNING
> - TAKE A SIP OF PERSONALIZED LEARNING

Project-Based Learning

You've likely heard of PBL, but some of you may be wondering what it really is. It might be helpful to start with what it's not. For example, PBL is not simply a project at the end of a unit. It's not the extra special addition, the dessert at the end of the meal (credit to Tom Berger and PBLWorks, for that metaphor). It is, in fact, the opposite; PBL should be the main course. PBL is the vehicle for learning. PBL allows students to solve real-world problems and challenges. And when they engage in this meaningful work, students experience deeper learning (PBLWorks, n.d.)

We will offer a short primer on this meaningful approach, but know there are many great organizations and resources out there. Some folks will say that PBL is not rigorous or real learning, particularly those that excelled in traditional, memorization, or lecture-based schooling. This could not be further from the truth. High-quality PBL is more rigorous, involving many more transferable skills than memorization, testing, and lecture require. The best part? You as a teacher FEEL better when students are not doing disposable, shallow, or memorization-based work. When students are invested in projects they care about, it is contagious. It helps your spirit as well.

> PBL is about preparing students for the unpredictable, collaborative, and creative demands of the real world.
>
> —PBLWorks (n.d.)

PBL includes an authentic audience sharing opportunity and this can be dramatically powerful. Students come together with other students, their families, and often community groups and the public to share their important work. This kind of sharing has many benefits. In one school we know, eighth graders interviewed "local heroes." They identified a local person to interview and developed their own interview questions (a powerful learning experience in and of itself). After the interview was complete, they worked with their humanities teachers through a revision process to bring the piece to a final draft. In art class, they used a photograph of their local hero as the basis for creating a wood-carved portrait of them. The students completed these original art pieces to put alongside their written pieces. Next, students asked the owners of a local coffee shop if they would host an art show and opening of these powerful pieces. On a very cold winter night, the local heroes and their eighth grade interviewers came out and celebrated their community and connection! Not only were the elders and local heroes honored and celebrated, but they were able to view the students in a positive light, as productive community members. Students felt seen and valued. It was an event that brought a community together. Students are motivated by sharing with an audience that matters to them. They build key communication skills and experience from this, and also grow deep positive connections with their local communities. This is the power of PBL.

Service Learning
Another teacher we know developed a rich service learning program that benefits his school's community in significant ways. Concerned about the decline in student engagement and mental health from the pandemic, this teacher knew his students needed to step away from screens and do something with their hands, do something that made a difference to their local community. He created space in the curriculum for his students to learn to grow food, cook with it, package it, deliver it directly to nearby food shelves, and connect this learning to the concepts of sustainability and civic engagement. The students make bread, pesto, salads, and meals, and then walk downtown themselves to deliver their efforts to the local food bank and to a free community refrigerator. Students have pride in this work, work that serves their own town and its citizens. We think this curriculum is a great example of service learning. Service learning can help students grow personally, in the areas of empathy, compassion, community, and engagement. Many of the things the pandemic took away from kids.

What is service learning? We like this KIDS Consortium's definition,

> *When students discover problems and needs in their school; investigate the causes and effects of the problems they identify; research various solutions to the problems; evaluate the pros and cons of each solution and decide on the actions to take; create an action plan and timeline to implement ideas; implement the plan; and evaluate the results of actions.*
>
> (Kaye & Associates, 2002, p. 3)

But to take this a step forward, and connect service learning to culturally responsive teaching, we encourage you to consider critical service learning. This approach applies social justice principles to service learning so it deepens and extends the work, and doesn't reinforce stereotypes or hierarchies. "A critical service-learning pedagogy links service-learning and social justice education by engaging students in meaningful service in the community and integrating that experience with thoughtful introduction, analysis, and discussion of issues important to understanding social justice" (Mitchell, 2007, p. 101). Of course, communities don't need saviors, especially those who don't know or understand the communities they are in. It is important in service learning to focus first on what is right and good about a community, place, school, and area.

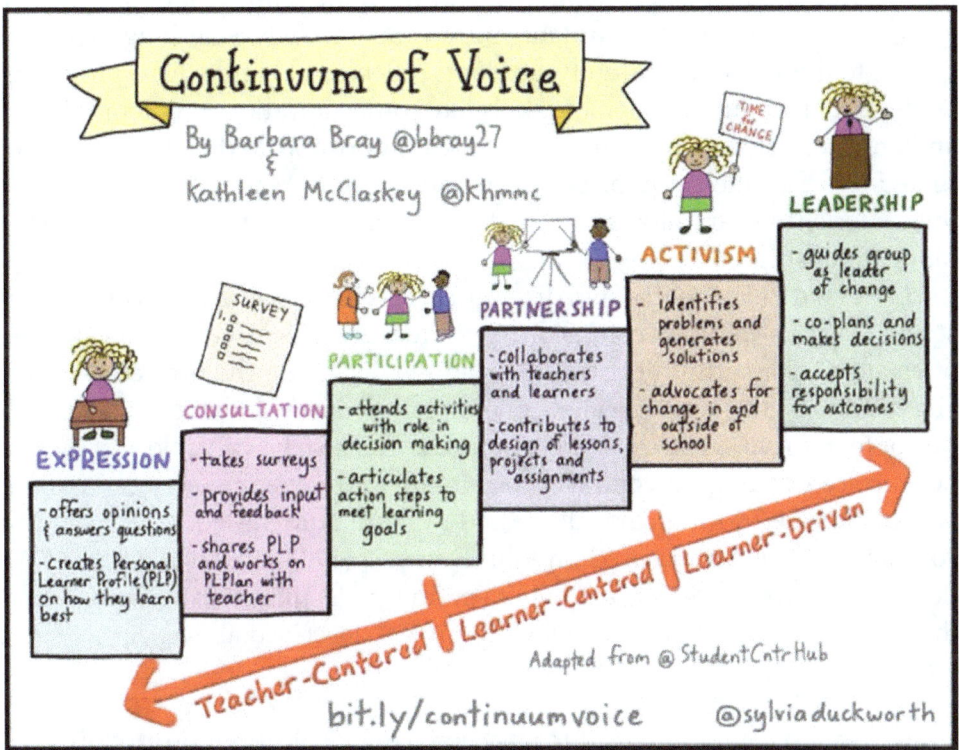

Figure 5.1 Bray and McClaskey's Continuum of Voice.

High-quality service learning is student-led (Figure 5.1). Students learn about their own local and global communities. They identify issues, assets, and problems. They (with teacher guidance, and a content or standards focus) figure out how to improve a condition or help to solve a problem. They create an action plan, identify materials needed, and create timelines and to-do lists. Students make the phone calls, send the emails to community groups. With support from community groups, local leaders and resources, and trusted sources, students connect local and global issues to social justice and change, focusing on how to build civic skills and become participating members of a community.

Here's an example of sixth graders who participated in a service learning and leadership project. During the unit, students explored their own passions and developed resumes that highlighted their experiences and interests. Simultaneously, the school faculty and staff created a list of community needs and jobs that students could perform. The faculty and staff created job postings (help wanted!) for positions such as Physical Education helper, reading buddy, school sports reporter, school photographer, chef's assistant, and school tour guide, and posted them in the sixth grade classroom. Students applied for these positions with their cover letters and resumes, and were interviewed by their teacher and a mentor from the school community. Once awarded the position, the students began their weekly year-long "jobs" of service to the school community. Students reflected along the way, providing evidence of meeting transferable skills like communication, problem solving, and engaged citizenship. Students created a portfolio of this work and presented it to the whole school as a culminating event. Years later, we hear that this experience sparked a career goal, a college major, or a lifelong community relationship!

Let's take a brief moment to distinguish service learning from community service, as it's a common confusion. Community service, while also valuable, often stems from adult decisions. The adults decide on the projects, actions, and outcomes. It's also typically a one-and-done event, like the isolated bake sale or food drive. To be clear, those activities can also be valuable. But they're not service learning. In contrast, meaningful and engaging service learning is explicitly tied to the curriculum and is more student-led. It is rooted in constant reflection and based on John Dewey's (1933) observation that "We do not learn from experience … we learn from reflecting on experience." And that was a key aspect of this leadership project described above.

> The greatest sign of success for a teacher is to be able to say, "The children are now working as if I did not exist."
> —Maria Montessori (1967)

Service learning can help to build community and mend fractures. Student-led events that feature the positives of a community, such as project presentations, speeches, art exhibits, and other community events led by students as part of their schooling increases meaning, purpose, and connection for both students and teachers. It also helps the community see the incredible things happening at the school, grows support for the school, and places young people in a positive light, contrasting with the all-too-common negative stereotypes they're subjected to on a regular basis. Telling and sharing a community's stories, showcasing its assets, working toward making it better, and celebrating progress all provide opportunities for a community to come together and create an authentic and appreciative audience for students.

To get into the weeds of this, you'll need – and find – plenty of resources out in the world. We've listed a few at the end of this chapter. But here's the kicker. When you do this work, you FEEL good. You see your students feeling good. And you know you have done something not only to help them, but to help your community AND connect people who are engaged in positive work. What's more, the people in the community begin looking at your students in new ways. Hey, young people today don't just stare at their phones and play video games! They are citizens of the world who are capable of helping. And that is meaningful.

Personalized Learning

Personalized learning is another avenue into meaningful curriculum. Personalized learning is rooted in a partnership between students and teachers, in which they co-design learning based on students' interests, needs, and questions (Bray & McClaskey, 2015. Too often people equate personalized learning with something that is hyper-individualized and technology dependent. We want to make clear that the best personalization is both personal and social, filled with purpose, and rooted in community. And yes, we can definitely leverage technology in lots of ways, including customizing learning pathways and managing the extraordinary amount of assessment data that is generated. But high-quality personalized learning should be evaluated by the learning and engagement, not by the technology employed (Bishop et al., 2020).

Research shows that teachers adopt varied roles when creating personalized learning environments. No more sage on the stage. In personalized learning, teachers become empowerers, scouts, scaffolders, and assessors (Bishop et al., 2020). Teachers facilitate learning, focusing on ways to support students in their quest for new skills and knowledge (Figure 5.2).

If you think about it, many of the approaches we describe here are highly personalized, and these roles are essential and inherent to that kind of approach, which can be a lot more fun than a simple lecture to students. For example, students might have personalized goals in mathematics that involve a student taking an assessment on the computer, setting goals, and developing a plan to meet them through various approaches, including collaborative problem solving, online personalized practice, math journaling, and other approaches. All of which are tailored to the students' goals and needs. At Katy's former elementary school, students have access to personalized learning during their math menu time. This is an interactive, engaging part of a

Figure 5.2 Teacher Roles in Personalized Learning Environments (Singh, 2024).

math lesson, where students have choice on many activities, and these can be personalized and differentiated to the student. During math menu, students play math games, work on puzzles and collaborative problem solving, enjoy integrated art and math projects, and meet with the teacher for support. These activities change based on students' needs, interests, mindsets, and skills.

Place-Based Learning

Meaningful curriculum often centers around place. Who lives here? Who has lived here? Why does this place matter? How does this place impact the lives of those in our community? Every place and community has something to connect to. A nearby business, garden, stream, or park. Whether it's focused on a rock wall or a city block, place-based learning connects students deeply to the place where they live. Writer David Sobel describes place-based education as

> *the process of using the local community and environment as a starting point to teach concepts in language arts, mathematics, social studies, science and other concepts across the curriculum. Emphasizing hands-on, real-world learning experiences, this approach to education increases academic achievement, helps students develop stronger ties to their community, enhances students' appreciation for the natural world, and creates a heightened commitment to serving as active, contributing citizens.*
>
> (Sobel, 2004, p. 7)

One benefit of place-based learning is that it often gets teachers and students out of the school building. We know that getting students outside is beneficial for their mental health and, with solid norms and outdoor procedures, this can be refreshing and enlivening for teachers as well. Eric Walters applied this teaching approach to his AP Physics classes, asking students to "engage students in their physical environment by encouraging them to ask physics-based questions about their surroundings" (2024). He invited students to explore their local communities through a Science, Technology, Engineering, Mathematics (STEM) lens, developing a series of educational videos for the community to engage in STEM learning. His students have created walking tours of Central Park and East Harlem. The project features student choice and exploration, as students look for physics-related examples in their communities and photograph them. They then develop observable questions and seek to answer it through research. Finally, students develop a 90-second educational video for the public via Google Earth for worldwide access (Walters, 2024). Now that's a physics class we'd love to take!

Maker Education

> We are born makers. We move what we're learning from our heads to our hearts through our hands.
>
> —Brené Brown (2015, p. 196)

Humans are inherent makers. From our earliest play, we create elaborate worlds and inventions. Can you remember any of your own creations? Too often this door gets locked as students stop seeing themselves as makers or as they decide they just aren't "STEM people." What if we kept the door open for them? Provided open times for creating? What if we reminded them that everyone is a maker, not just those who build rockets? School can be a place where kids learn to sew, code, use a 3D printer, and repair items for the community. They can make circuits that show something about themselves and invent things to help others. Maker education and design thinking are approaches for you to learn more about if this intrigues you.

Start with a process that takes students on a journey through emphasizing (where students learn about the people – or animals – they are designing for); defining an issue (based on needs); ideating (brainstorming solutions); prototyping (creating a model of a solution); and testing (trying out the product and getting feedback) (Shanks, n.d.). Makerspaces are defined as "a place that provides hands-on, creative ways for students to design, experiment, and invent as they engage with a variety of tools and technology. Multidisciplinary both in approach and in the products created, makerspaces fuels engagement and innovation" (Xavier University, n.d.).

"A makerspace is a space for creating and making. The term 'makerspaces' conjures up different images in almost everybody who uses it. A makerspace can be many different things. Makerspaces can have all types of tools, supplies, and equipment" (Farber, 2018).
Makerspaces can be created most anywhere. And in recent years, more and more schools are finding spaces to include them, even as an idea if not a physical space. For example, we know a school librarian and principal who developed a year-long STEAM (science, technology, engineering, art, and math) course for their students. This K-5 class was a 45-minute block of STEAM time that focused on connecting to the local community and global sustainability efforts (Global Goals, read on, will discuss below!). This program also included a sometimes missing part of STEM efforts: empathy. During each STEAM time, students worked through Stanford's five phases of design thinking: Empathize, Define, Ideate, Prototype, Test.

One great example from that program was the Fairytale Engineering unit. Students were asked to take a familiar fairy tale and use STEAM to solve some of the problems in the stories.

- **Empathize:** The principal read students a fairytale, asking them to consider the story from various viewpoints.
- **Define:** In pairs, students asked each other, "What did you see?" and identified the types of problems the characters faced.
- **Ideate:** Students used the library's white board tables to brainstorm ideas for ways that engineering or creating could help the characters solve their problems.
- **Prototype**: Students chose a solution and got to work with the art and making supplies.

- **Test:** Students tested and presented their prototypes to the class for feedback. Some students designed ways Jack could carry his golden eggs to safety; others crafted ways for Rapunzel to safely leave her tower without having to get married! (Farber, 2018.).

Civic Education

No matter what their age, children are citizens of our local, national, and global communities. They can develop key skills to think critically and be informed, empathetic voters and participants in our democracy. The Annenberg Classroom defines civic education as

teaching the knowledge, skills, and virtues needed for competent citizenship in a democracy. Unlike despotic forms of government in which the people are merely passive receivers of orders from their rulers, democracy involves a significant measure of independent thinking and popular decision-making. A democracy cannot be maintained unless the citizens are educated sufficiently to carry out certain duties and responsibilities of a self-governing people, such as voting intelligently, communicating effectively about public issues, cooperating with others to solve common problems, and making judgments about the performance of their government. (Annenberg Classroom, n.d.)

Public education plays a key role (and ever increasingly important role) in this process. So what does it look like?

Meaningful curriculum often ties to the news – what is happening around students. Every single day there's a constant stream of local, state, national, and global news. Of course, these articles are not always developmentally appropriate for younger students, but we have lots of tools that make the news accessible for students at any level, such as *NewsELA* and *Time for Kids*. When we ignore the news, we ignore the current realities, student interests, and local contexts. In this era of too much mis- and dis-information, it's also a great opportunity for teaching media literacy. How do we tell truth from fiction? How do we evaluate the veracity of our sources? How can we find reliable, factual information? Luckily, there are great resources out there for teaching media literacy at all ages. We've listed a few in the Dig Deeper section below.

Consider reading and discussing news that feels important to your students. Advisory or morning meetings are a good time for this. Doing so helps your students see futures for themselves as civically engaged, knowledgeable citizens who are capable of positive change. And when you pair this with service learning or place-based learning, the sky's the limit! We highly recommend engaging with the 17 Global Goals for Sustainable Development showcased in Figure 5.3.

Figure 5.3 Global Goals.

Credit: Reprinted with permission. The content of this publication has not been approved by the United Nations and does not reflect the views of the United Nations or its officials or Member States. Learn more at https://www.un.org/sustainabledevelopment/.

Developed by the United Nations' member countries, they are a collection vision for a better world through 17 powerful goals. Because of this, they provide a ready framework for meaningful work! Goals such as good health and well-being, no poverty, life on land, and sustainable communities connect to multiple disciplines and provide immediate access to others working on these issues (Global Goals, n.d). We've seen students as young as those in kindergarten identify Global Goals in picture books and interact online with professionals working toward these goals. We've also seen eighth graders "dot storm" the Global Goals (using small dot stickers on chart paper to categorize the goals based on interests and importance) as a springboard for PBL rooted in their interests, local needs, and community organizations. In both cases, students are building an understanding of what it means to be part of a global community working for positive change.

We know that you're teaching in a political context. Like it or not, the politics around us influence what and how we teach. And in US schools and communities, political divisiveness feels at an all-time high. Working toward the common good of our world helps students connect to their sense of shared humanity. Importantly, it helps them see how they can make a positive change in the world around them. Leading meaningful learning that connects students to their communities can help to heal the damage from the pandemic and also bridge vast political divides.

> Caring involves stepping out of one's own personal frame of reference into the other's.
>
> —Nel Noddings (1984)

In short, meaningful curriculum is about more than merely engaging students. It is about expanding the world of school and about connecting deeply to communities, place, and purpose. Yes, this work can be challenging. The classroom can feel loud and messy sometimes. But it can also be deeply moving for educators. Research tells us that *meaning* can be a protective factor, improving our health and even working to prevent burnout. In fact, a greater sense of purpose was associated with a 17% lower risk of all cause mortality (Roepke et al., 2014). So we like to think that doing meaningful work with students can literally help save your own life! In addition, being part of the education system is working toward something larger than yourself. This, in and of itself, makes for a more meaningful life, which in turn helps us thrive in good times and manage the difficult ones (Nagoski & Nagoski, 2019). Meaningful teaching and learning provides joy, purpose, and efficacy – all of which help prevent burnout and promote a long, healthy, fulfilled life, which we wish for every one of you!

Dig Deeper

- **Check out** PBLWorks: https://my.pblworks.org/
- **View** these Toolkits: https://tiie.w3.uvm.edu/blog/project-based-learning-2/
- **Read** (shameless plug!) *Personalized Learning in the Middle Grades*, by Penny Bishop, John Downes, and Katy Farber, 2019, Harvard Education Press and *Real and Relevant: A guide to service and project-based learning* by Katy Farber, 2017, Rowman and Littlefield.
- **Read** *Culturally Responsive and Community-Focused PBL*: https://www.edutopia.org/article/culturally-responsive-project-based-learning
- **Explore** Media Literacy Resources
  - Free Classroom Resources for Teaching the Constitution: https://www.annenbergclassroom.org/
  - What is Media Literacy and How Can Simple Shifts Center it, from Public Broadcasting Service (PBS): https://www.pbs.org/education/blogs/pbs-in-the-classroom/what-is-media-literacy-and-how-can-simple-shifts-center-it/
- **Listen** to Hidden Brain, You 2.0 Fighting Despair: https://hiddenbrain.org/podcast/you-2-0-fighting-despair/

 **Reflect, Dream, Plan**

- What appetizer was tastiest? Which of the six approaches resonated with you most as you read this chapter?
- Which other ones are you curious about? Which do you think will spark joy and meaning in your learners and in yourself?
- Which ideas might work best in your particular school content or community?
- What approaches might you want to explore further?
- What excites you about a particular approach?
- What ideas for meaningful instruction percolated for you during this chapter? Write or sketch them below!

Build Your Playlist

What song about meaning and purpose will help motivate you?

Identify Your Big Three

Okay, it's time! List your BIG THREE from this chapter. What are three steps you can take to dial up the engagement and meaning in your classroom and community? Draw or list below.

1.

2.

3.

6

Building Community with Students

Chapter Overview

When you think back on your schooling, we bet a few teachers come to mind. Those who asked about your sports team, or your family, or pets, or maybe the issues that were important to you. You'll hear people say it's all about relationships in teaching. And they're right! Without building strong relationships with your students, teaching them anything can be a major challenge. This chapter will explore the many ways to connect with students, build trust and community, and lay the essential foundation for learning.

> To teach in a manner that respects and cares for the souls of our students is essential if we are to provide the necessary conditions where learning can most deeply and intimately begin.
>
> —bell hooks (1994)

Connect

Katy's classroom had adopted a "soft start" norm. As they entered the room, students could take a few moments to get settled, read, draw, or chat. One year, Katy had a student who particularly loved horror movies, violent video games, and drawing monsters. He would come into the classroom with his head down, grab a piece of paper, and start drawing the most intense, detailed, and creepiest monster you've ever seen. He would have done it all day if she'd let him.

Katy knew she had her work cut out for her. First of all, she couldn't identify any shared interests. Horror movies were the opposite of how she wanted to spend her time, and she held a strong bias against video games, which she felt could desensitize kids against violence. At the same time, he was her student. It was her job to connect with him, provide a safe place for learning, and welcome him into a supportive community.

Katy needed to focus on what was good, on his assets, not his supposed flaws. She reminded herself that, simply by walking through the classroom door, the student deserved her unconditional positive regard. We spend more time on this idea in Chapter 8, but essentially "Unconditional Positive Self-Regard" is a way of being with students, expressing to them that "I care about you. You have value. You don't have to do anything to prove it to me, and nothing's going to change my mind" (Venet, 2023, p. 98). The fact that the student might draw all day, or throw the paper to the ground, or swear, didn't change that. Katy reminded herself that behavior is a form of communication. He was trying to communicate something and it was up to her to figure out what.

So first, she marveled at the drawings. She showed genuine interest. They really were incredible. And she continued to let him draw in the mornings. Yes, it was a struggle to get him to stop sometimes. After they built up a little trust, she asked if he'd like to showcase his illustrations so others could see them. He started sharing them with other students at morning meetings, while Katy reserved the right to veto weapons or other things she deemed too creepy for the other students. Next, she suggested he make a book of these illustrations. Their relationship, while not easy, became rooted in his strengths and interests. Katy's goal became helping him feel seen and valued in a system where he hadn't experienced much of that. These were a series of small moves, but they made a large difference. He did make that book and was proud to share it. If he keeps it up, he may create the next Coraline or The Addams Family. It all starts with relationships.

> If you're feeling frustrated or stymied, remember that student growth takes time; each day builds on the day before. You have so many chances each day to try a different approach. Don't beat yourself up – try a different way. Also, I find it useful to be less worried and more curious, although it took a while to get there!
> —Valerie Bang-Jensen, Professor of Education Emerita

Real Talk

> Students don't care how much you know until they know how much you care.
>
> —Anonymous

Get to Know Students

Everything starts with what students care about. It turns out, students are already whole people! They have all sorts of interesting interests and experiences. The first six weeks of school are vital for discovering student interests and building a strong relationship. This task can feel daunting, but many schools have adopted programs (like advisories, Responsive Classroom, Developmental Designs, and Conscious Discipline) that explicitly address community building and social emotional skills. If you're in a school with a program, lean into it. Remember too that, while those first few weeks are critical, this is a year-long endeavor.

No program? No problem. Here are a few ideas to get you pointed in the right direction.

As with most things, the best way to start is using common sense. Smile, say hello at the door, welcome students in, and begin a low-stakes conversation about anything. It could be the novel or sketchbook they're holding, a sports team logo on their hat, or something else you notice. You'll likely find a way to connect with more than 85% of your students through simple observation and conversation. Some students may not want to engage right away, so be patient. You don't want to overwhelm them. Just show a continued, calm, and curious interest.

For that other 15%, consider more focused observation. Act like a researcher. Often it is students' behavior, rather than their words, that communicates their needs; not what they say, but what they do. How are they presenting? Do they seem nervous or self-conscious? Are they acting out to get attention? Or are they trying to fly under the radar? At the same time, be careful not to jump to conclusions. Remember that their behavior might not be the same as yours in similar situations. This may especially be true for students who have experienced trauma. Take some notes on what you notice. This will help you think about how to develop a positive connection.

You can speed things up with student interest inventories. No need to reinvent the wheel (remember that subtraction we talked about in Chapter 2?), as these are widely found. They vary quite a bit in quality, so perhaps start with those listed in our resources. You can also create one on Google Forms.

Favorite foods, teams, activities, places, pets are all great places to begin. However you do it, begin the conversation.

> "Make kindness your first priority in each of your interactions with students. Even when the job is tough, showing them that you're on their side makes everything much easier."
> —Alden Ducharme, Middle School Math Teacher

You can also inventory students' learning preferences. You've probably heard of learning styles. The concept that some students are visual, some are auditory, and others kinesthetic gained popularity in the 1990s. You might even think of yourself in these ways. And while some aspects of that are helpful, research has found this to be quite limiting (Reiner & Willingham, 2010). It is not that simplistic. It is more about having multiple ways of representation, often called multimodal learning. Providing visual, written, auditory, social, and movement representations for learning. Why? Because students have different learning preferences, and these are important. Also, students arrive with different challenges (and strengths!). So it's helpful to learn about them and learning preference inventories are a great way to do this. You can find examples in our resource section or design your own. While these are always good to know, providing a range of access points to learning is key to working effectively with any group of students.

Getting to know students as whole people can also mean selecting a few times to work a little more than usual. Attend a basketball game, a dance recital, or another event after school hours to connect with a student or family. This is not something to be done lightly, because you'll want to make sure you have enough (or a passable amount) of downtime, but a little effort here can go a LONG way. Students notice when you show up for them. Even if they don't say anything at the time, it is noticed and builds trust. So, show up for extra things when you can, but not at the expense of your health and well-being. Make sense?

PERMISSION SLIP

YOU ARE HEREBY GRANTED PERMISSION TO:
- LAUGH WITH YOUR STUDENTS
- FOLLOW THEIR INTERESTS
- BE RIDICULOUSLY SILLY WITH THEM
- ASK OTHERS FOR HELP WITH HOW TO CONNECT WITH A STUDENT

Finally, remember that you're not alone as you begin these relationships. Think about what you've observed. Does the student head off to a dance class, sports team, or club after school? Confer with the trusted adult running the program. Does the student work after school? Ask how they spent their afternoon time and consult with others. They might have some insights for you. Previous teachers also hold important information. Unfortunately, we often hear things like "Oh, wait until you get this student!" or "You are going to have a lot of fun with this student," with sarcastic tone included. These comments are spectacularly unhelpful. Nothing about this helps us understand the student and think about how to connect with them. On the contrary, it invites us to make pre-conceived (and often ill-conceived) assumptions about students. But sitting down with last year's teacher can be very helpful if the focus is on planning for or improving a transition. You don't want students to have to explain themselves to you, especially if there has been trauma or significant challenges in prior years. This is precisely when a quick meeting with the last year's teacher can prove useful. Invite the former teacher to provide a summary of the student, including their interests, challenges, and anything they think will help you build a positive relationship. You can often get some great tips and ideas here.

> Remember that 99% of the time kids' emotions and reactions are not because they dislike the teacher; it's 100 other things they are going and growing through.
> —Honi Bean Barrett, Fifth and Sixth Grade Teacher

Be Flexible

> To guide your reactions when working with students, always consider, "Based on their emotional state and behavior, what does the student need in this moment? Do they need to know they are safe, they are loved, or what can they learn?" Respond in a way that aligns with that current need. You will have incredible success connecting with and coregulating with students!
> —Special Educator

When building community with students, consider using the mantra: *New Day, New Chance*. Let go of what happened the day before. This one is hard, but essential. Give your students a new chance each day to start over.

Treat each day as a new beginning, a new chance to learn and connect. Show that you care about them inherently. It is refreshed each day. (We'll tell you more about this concept of unconditional positive regard in Chapter 8.) This can be hard if you haven't processed feelings about what happened the day before. That is why it is important to tend to your own feelings and reactions first, by working through them by talking to others, exercising, resting, or reflecting. But each day? It is a clean slate.

Similarly, try to be flexible. If you like control, and order, and quiet, teaching can be particularly hard. Especially in those first years. Everything seems challenging. But, if you try to hold on to a mindset of flexibility, you may find yourself feeling better. Identify your non-negotiables, and keep it a short list.

What do we mean? Well, is it really a problem if that student works on the floor? Or if another does the math problems in a different order? How about the student who does a quick sketch on the side of the paper, or the one who needs another pencil or snack? Identify what really matters. What are your non-negotiables? Decide what is actually important and worth your energy and time. If you are calm and relaxed, and you can give students some choice and flexibility, you will also feel more at ease. This doesn't mean allowing for chaos! Rather, it means picking your battles, offering humanity and choice, and holding a mindset of flexibility.

> People will forget what you said, people will forget what you did, but people will never forget how you made them feel.
> —Maya Angelou (1987)

Be Trauma-Informed

Perhaps you've taken a class in trauma-informed practices, or maybe you've heard of them. Like many concepts in education, trauma-informed education has different definitions and the term is widely used (sometimes in shallow, performative ways). We like how Alex Shevrin Venet defines it:

> *Trauma-informed educational practices respond to the impacts of trauma on the entire school community and prevent future trauma from occurring. Equity and social justice are key concerns of trauma-informed educators as we make change in our individual practice in classrooms, in schools, and in district-wide and state-wide systems.*
>
> (2023, p. 10)

Venet connects equity and trauma-informed practices by inviting educators to pose the question, "Does this practice, policy, or decision help or harm students from marginalized communities? (p.12)."

We all want to build a safe and caring environment for students to thrive. But how can we do that? Venet outlines several principles. First, trauma-informed practices must be anti-oppressive. Trauma can happen at school, especially racialized harm. So it is important that schools do not perpetuate harm and actively seek to eliminate inequity in school which causes trauma. Second, education must be asset-based, focused on student strengths rather than their perceived deficits. We aren't in the business of "fixing" kids. We are working to improve the conditions, environments, and systems they are in. Next, Shevrin Venet asserts that trauma-informed practice must be a human-centered, systems approach, where the safe environment and the practices are embedded across a system. Trauma-informed approaches are universal (for all students) and proactive (not only implemented after a trauma occurs). Lastly, trauma-informed approaches are social justice-oriented because the goal is to live in a just, safe, and trauma-free world (Venet, 2023).

One year, Katy had selected a read-aloud book that had a fire event in it. One student let her know that she'd lost a family member in a fire. Katy abandoned the book and picked another. Another student confided that a popular song was unbearable; it reminded her of her grandmother who recently passed away. They immediately took it off the class playlist. These are just two examples of responsive practice that honors students. Your students will show you the way if you build trusting relationships with them.

What might this look like in *your* teaching practice? It looks like addressing your students' needs beyond academics and looking out for their whole person. Noticing who has warm clothes and who does not. Who brings a snack every day and who doesn't. Knowing your students' families, interests, and previous experiences in school. Challenging one-size-fits-all policies or programs that are shared at staff meetings. Offering a guaranteed clean slate each day. Creating a classroom climate based on respect, inclusion, and community. It looks like holding a steadfast belief in the student and their potential.

> Strive to create spaces and moments that align with the way that you wish the world could be and by giving students a glimpse of those possibilities, you will show them that they can and deserve to truly thrive.
> —Life LeGeros, Civics & Equity Teacher

Listen Actively

We know. It's hard. Your to-do list is as long as your arm and then a student appears in front of you, wanting to tell you all about an elaborate dream. Or maybe it's a video game. Or something else that matters to them. It's tempting to keep grading papers, moving your eyes from the computer, to your desk and back again. Not looking up at the student, trying to power through because, perhaps, report cards are due at the end of the day. But we also know that behavior is communication, and every student wants to be seen and heard.

You can set certain limits such as "Please tell me more about that at recess!" but the big idea here is to flex your active listening skills. This is key to building community with students. It begins with listening and really seeing your students. Pausing. Noticing their habits, listening to their stories. Some students don't have anyone in their lives who does this fully. You very well might be the only one. Ask open-ended questions. Try not to interrupt or offer advice (oh so hard). Practice empathy by trying to understand their perspective, especially if it's very different from your own. Even if you have very little bandwidth, thank them for sharing with you, and promise to circle back at another time.

Model Vulnerability (But Don't Overshare!)

If you've read any Brené Brown, you'll know that vulnerability is an important bridge to build connection (2010). As you work to build community with your students, think about the role that vulnerability can play. First, admitting when you have made a mistake is a key way to normalize mistake-making as learning. It shows that you are human and fallible, not other than and "perfect." Likewise, telling students a story of your own failure can build connections and model how to get back up from life struggles. Katy's students loved to hear about her baking failures for example (how could you forget the flour?!). It can also lead to a "yet" environment, where students hear you describe something you can't do *yet*. Another approach is to admit when you don't know something. It doesn't matter what it's about – geography, current events, or a math term. Let students know that you are unsure and model how to seek accurate information. You can find out together. This illustrates lifelong learning as a way of being. Similarly, show them how you can pause and reflect on your emotions. Labeling an emotion, then a pause, can help students connect to you and give themselves permission as well. "I am disappointed that the field trip is canceled, but I bet we can figure out something fun to do together." Consider inviting students' perspectives about your practice as well. This models constant growth, gives students a voice, and helps them know that they have a voice in their learning, and that you are strong and vulnerable enough to hear their feedback. While all this vulnerability talk is great, there are plenty of boundaries here. Vulnerability with students does *not* mean sharing personal details of your life that are inappropriate for school and your students. Talking about the antics of your cute cat? Great! Photographs of your evening out with friends? Definitely not. Show students your humanity while maintaining a healthy boundary. You got this.

Dig Deeper

- **Visit** this link to explore the *First 20 Days of Personalized Learning*. This guide has a great set of approaches and activities for the first 20 days of school that can help you both build relationships AND make connections. https://www.edelements.com/first-20-days-of-personalized-learning
- **Check out** this Hyperdoc. Teaching virtually? You can still build strong relationships! Here is a Hyperdoc with built-in Google Forms related to feelings and the movie Inside Out: https://hyperdocs.co/blog/posts/strategies-to-support-the-social-emotional-development-of-students
- **Read** this *We Are Teachers* post. This post is a helpful list of things you can do to keep your students (and yourself!) well and connect with them. https://www.weareteachers.com/build-healthy-student-minds/
- **Write** letters to your students in the summer. Some teachers write postcards to each student over the summer. Actual postcards! Actual mail! Imagine the excitement that causes for kids (anyone, really). While this is time-consuming, it has a big impact. Consider this a form of summer connection. https://www.edutopia.org/article/building-relationships-through-letter-writing
- **Review** some student learning preference surveys: https://possibilitiesforlearning.com/learning-preference-survey/
- **Read** *Equity-Centered Trauma-Informed Education* by Alex Shevrin Venet

Reflect, Dream, Plan

To begin, imagine what it will look and feel like to have positive, strong relationships with your students.

- What will it feel like?
- How might you build community and trust with your students? What resonates? What might you or have you tried? List or draw here.

Building Community with Students ◆ 79

Build Your Playlist

What song motivates you to build strong relationships and learn about your students' lives?

What activities or assignments will you do that helps to build community?

Identify Your Big Three

From the reflections above, select your Big Three. What approaches to building relationships will you practice?

   1.

   2.

   3.

7

Building Community with Families

Chapter Overview

Families and caregivers are children's first teachers. They know their children well and can be a bank of knowledge about your students. Families and caregivers want what is best for their child, even if at times you may disagree about what "best" means. This chapter will help you shape an approach to engaging with families, consider your boundaries, and help you build relationships that support your students.

Connect

At the start of a new school year, our friend Natalia planned to use a digital program called Seesaw as her regular way to communicate and engage with parents and caregivers of her kindergarteners throughout the year. She knew, however, that most families would benefit from an introduction to the software. She also knew that the introduction couldn't wait until the fall Open House; by that time families would have missed important messages and updates about their young children transitioning to kindergarten. Most of these parents were working full-time jobs, sometimes more than one. Many of them were new Americans. And all of them were busy people. So Natalia set up coffee/tea and technology times in the morning before school. During these sessions, family members could grab a donut while getting support for downloading the app to their phones. This time was a great investment. The parents were able to see the updates from the classroom immediately as soon as they were updated. There is nothing like getting a picture or video of your child's smile and work in real time!

To be sure, Natalia's approach was time-intensive at the start. But it saved time as the year unfolded. Through the app, Natalia could easily post photos, permission slips, schedule updates, surveys, and more. Easy-peasy. The students used iPads to post their work regularly, proudly sharing their work with families and connecting almost every day. The community, the trust, and the access, all grew from this set of moves on the teacher's part. Natalia's approach is a great example of the kind of frontloading we talked about in Chapter 2. Time spent collaborating with families is a key investment in your and students' success.

Real Talk

Effective family-teacher partnerships are central to students' success. For that reason, just as you routinely spend time planning your work with students, so too it is helpful to consider how you engage with families. After all, families and caregivers hold unique vantage points and insights into their children. They know their children's histories, their assets, their struggles, and their preferences.

Start with the Positive

> Be proactive, and reach out to families for a positive reason as soon as you can. When dealing with challenges, frame them in the form of "let's work on this together," with the student's success as the goal.
> —Forest Matthews, High School Work Based Learning Teacher

Some people consider family engagement to be only an "elementary school thing." We disagree. While it may look different across the tiers of schooling, building meaningful relationships with families is important for all teachers. Because it's helpful for all students.

At the beginning of the year, plan to be in touch regularly with families. Consider how you will communicate regularly. Will you use a weekly email or newsletter? Text or website? Something else? Make a sustainable plan for this and start right away. This helps to build trust, connection, and community. Even if some parents never engage with it, you've opened the door.

We suggest you identify a streamlined way to communicate with families as a group. For example, set up your Google email group, or other way of BCC-ing all families, and then send them greetings and information about the school year right away. It's especially helpful to make your first contact with families be a positive one. Take a bunch of photos (while attending to your school's media policies and families' consent) and insert them in a newsletter. Alternatively, send a special email with some photos and positive words about the class. You can also use whole group communication as a way to foster relationships between caregivers and their children. For example, provide families with a list of five questions to ask their child about. This helps caregivers avoid the dreaded "What did you do at school today?" "Nothing" exchange. Overall, try to focus on what is good and right with your class and the students. We don't mean toxic positivity. Be strengths-based. We're all more receptive to feedback once we know we are appreciated and valued.

Next, layer on your strategy for individual family communication. As you get to know the students, start sending out some short positive emails about individual students to their families. It's ok if it takes a while to get through the whole class list. This will pay back in huge relational dividends. And remember that communication is a two- (or three- or four-) way street. Families will benefit from knowing how to get in touch with you. Many families don't know that teachers may only have 20 minutes and no private spaces for calls. Or that it might be a whole school day or two before you can return a phone call. Be clear and specific about the best ways and times to reach you. Establish some communication boundaries. How do you want to communicate? When do you want to communicate? And then stick to those as much as possible. Remember those boundaries we discussed in Chapter 2? We know this will not always be possible, but we want you to make clear decisions and boundaries that support your health.

Learn from Families

> Start early and engage often. Positive communication home in the early weeks makes it so much easier to make harder conversations work later. Send out a survey asking parents about their child's likes, dislikes, how they learn best. You and caregivers are a team working together to support the child. Remember not every family dynamic is the same so be mindful of that.
>
> —Courtney Elliot, Fifth Grade Teacher

Your families know their child or children best. For the most part, they know what to do when the child is mad, what their triggers are, what their strengths are, and how best to reach them. Tap into this deep well of knowledge by surveying families in the first few weeks of school. A simple Google Form can tell you what language is spoken at home, what forms of communication the families prefer, and what the child's interests, strengths, and challenges are. Most families love to share this information and it illustrates immediately that you are working together for the success of the child.

While engagement is important for all families, they will inevitably have different levels of access. For some, there may be language, literacy, or technological barriers. Hopefully, your school has a system for informing you about some of these things. If not, find out what you can from last year's teachers. For example, if a language other than English is spoken at home, request assistance through your school to ensure your communications are accessible. If your district lacks those resources, leverage Google Translate or other AI technologies to help you translate. Similarly, make sure all families can access the digital system you're using. Some teachers, like Natalia at the start of this chapter, hold a coffee/drop-in time for parents to learn how to use a program like Seesaw or Google Classroom. Opportunities like this help to disarm the tools and make it easy to engage and stay in communication. Sending home quick "start up steps" notes and emails are a good way to do this too.

Engage in Parent/Family Conferences

Family engagement is a top concern of most new teachers, who typically report feeling underprepared in this area. For that reason, parent or family conferences might provoke a little anxiety. Conferences usually take place twice a year, and they're a wonderful opportunity to connect with families. So let's set you up for success.

First, while your regular emails or newsletters keep families informed on the regular, these conferences are a chance to go deeper. To prepare for these meetings, learn more about what conferences look like in your building and context. Feel free to lean on your mentors in the building to support you throughout this process. Ask questions. What are families in this school community accustomed to? Do other teachers have approaches that work well?

Next, let's acknowledge that many families are juggling multiple jobs. Consider being flexible with the timing and modality. You will help connect with more families if you can offer options regarding phone, Zoom, or in person, along with some variety in the dates and times. We've spoken with parents in line at the grocery store, met on Zoom, and come in before school for various conferences. Not all families are going to be able to make the one school day that the school gives you for these meetings.

Now consider what student-specific information you want to bring. Be sure to have some work to share with families (projects, papers, testing scores). Prior to the conference timing, you can invite students to reflect on how the semester is going and then share these reflections at the conference. What's working for them? What do they find challenging? And how are things going socially? Families care about these things, and what better way than to share the students' own words with them?

To kick off the conference, always begin with some positives about the student. Where do you see them shine? What are they interested in? Then share student reflections and student work, allowing the majority of time for dialogue and questions. Keep the time student-centered and solutions-oriented throughout. Convey the general idea that you are all on the same team, working to help the student. Use your active listening skills, and be ready to take notes on what needs following up on. You may think you'll remember that item for your to-do list, but if you have these conferences back-to-back, trust us, you won't.

After the conferences, take a moment to reflect. What went well? What might you want to change? This is a learning process. Eventually you may want to adopt a student-led conference model. Student-led conferences are just that. Students are present at the conference to lead the conversation. They showcase their reflections, progress, and work for their families. This can be a big challenge for students to present to their families, in terms of both their presentation skills and their vulnerability. But the meaningful conversations and connections are completely worth it. Students feel more a part of their education because the adults aren't talking *about* them, they are talking *with* them. Of course there are times when it is important that students not be present, to discuss difficult issues, for example, but these are often the exceptions. We have found it quite simple to state to the student that we'd like to chat for a few minutes directly with the family. There are lots of great resources if you are interested in student-led conferences, and we have one chock full of resources for you in the Dig Deeper section below.

> Start early and reach out often, and be curious. Remember you all want what is best for their kid, even if you may not agree on what that best is. So, show them you know and care about their kid, even if you have to call or email about a tricky situation, and then lead with curiosity. Do they have any ideas to help you? How does their child express frustration at home? What works to help them calm down?
> —Mike Rappoport, Fifth Grade Teacher

> **PERMISSION SLIP**
>
> YOU ARE HEREBY GRANTED PERMISSION TO:
>
> - NOT MAKE EVERYONE HAPPY
> - STAND BEHIND YOUR REASONING
> - NOT CHANGE YOUR MIND

We all get them. The long, maybe angry, email about something that happened at school. Or about something that happened in the past, with another teacher, in another year. Or perhaps it's a critique of something you are doing as a teacher. Sometimes it's even connected to the caregiver's own experience as a student.

It's easy to feel defensive right away. The temptation here is to bang out an email response immediately, with all that defensive and sometimes prickly energy. While it might feel good to write, this is definitely not what you should send. If you get this kind of email or voicemail, consider the following alternatives.

- ◆ Wait. Even 24 hours. Teach your classes, eat your dinner, go for a walk. Take some time for your nervous system to calm and reflect.
- ◆ Ponder. Think about the best way to respond. We have all gotten into long email exchanges that go nowhere. Would picking up the phone and having a human-to-human conversation be better? Or is email a safer way to control your own emotions?
- ◆ Consult. Bring the issue to your teaching team, trusted mentor, or colleague for some ideas about how to proceed. Ask a teacher who has a relationship with this student's family for ideas.

The main message here is to pause. Don't spend your energy and emotional health engaging until you feel calm, reflective, and ready. The 24-hour rule has definitely helped us manage our responses and develop stronger relationships with families.

When you do communicate, **lead with curiosity**. Welcome ideas that might be helpful in the situation. When caregivers feel like you are on the same team, they are more likely to open up and the discussion becomes more collaborative.

> When things seem challenging, try to come back to what you have in common: You both care about the well-being of the young person. Work hard to listen and understand their perspective, try not to be judgmental, and the go-to move during interactions is to repeat back what you've heard them say.
> —Life LeGeros, Civics and Equity Teacher

Be Prepared to Disagree

> Listen, be responsive, but don't feel the need to please everyone. You will not make everyone happy but if you have a good solid reason for doing something, be okay with standing behind it.
> —Michael Rappoport, Fifth Grade Teacher

Want to know an inalienable truth about education? Everyone's an expert. **Everyone who ever went to school has an opinion about how it's "supposed" to be**. This comes with the job. Some parents and caregivers will have contradictory opinions about the best way to teach. You may be seen as too strict or conversely as too free-wheeling. It may be that "old" math is better than "new" math (newsflash: it's not!). You may disagree about how to best teach reading. What to teach and when. The list goes on. If you've grown up as a people pleaser, this might be particularly hard for you.

We encourage you to remember that you and your colleagues are the experts here. You have studied and prepared for this career. You are knowledgeable about your school's curricular goals, standards, and practices. There is a difference between collaborating and asking for permission. You are

---

PERMISSION SLIP

YOU ARE HEREBY GRANTED PERMISSION TO:

- WAIT 24 HOURS BEFORE RESPONDING
- CONSULT WITH A COLLEAGUE
- TAKE A WALK AND PONDER

leading the class and the curriculum this year. So, put your shoulders back and stand tall. You might need to explain what the focus is and why, but do so in a short message. Sometimes parents will suggest things that are easy to change. If so, great! But if it's something you know goes against school guidelines, practices, policies, or research, or your students' needs and identities, thank the parent or caregiver for their feedback and let them know you appreciated hearing from them. If the issue escalates, it's time to rely on your principal and mentors to support you. Which brings us to… inviting support from others!

Invite Support

> You will absolutely have families that are difficult to work with during your career – some who are impossible to get a hold of, some who don't seem to care (though I'd argue that usually they just feel unequipped to help), and yes, sadly, occasionally just some terrible people because it's the world and there are just some bad apples, but 95% care and want to work with you, so don't let yourself be scared by the 5% or you miss out on the rich support that comes from the rest.
> —Triston Upson, Middle School English Language Arts Teacher

Sometimes you will need backup. After a few messages with the same parents, it's always good to check in with your principal and fill them in on some of the conversation. Ask for support if you need it. It's better to overcommunicate with building leaders in these cases. In fact, sometimes parents and caregivers will start with the building administrator, so it's possible they already know. At other times, you might be supported by specialists in the building, such as the school counselor, special educator, social worker, behaviorist, or reading or math interventionist. They can help you craft delicate communications, think through challenging matters, and brainstorm research-based solutions.

Know the Bottom Line

In today's divisive political climate, lots of folks have opinions about what you are reading and teaching. The bottom line is that all students need to feel seen, loved, and validated for who they are. This is job number one. This means validating *all* families and identities, regardless of different ideologies or political parties. Yes, all. Helping students feel a strong sense of belonging helps them fight depression, alleviate anxiety, and avoid self-harm. In some cases, it literally keeps them alive.

Know your school's mission statement. It likely includes language about helping every student to learn, be successful, and thrive as whole people. This is the work of schools. Rely on this and refer to it in your communications as needed. Have a copy or language nearby so you can use it if you need it.

If families are challenging your curriculum, find out why. Is a family concerned that something you did in class is potentially harmful in how it represents a group of people? Listen, reflect, process with colleagues, and make a more inclusive plan. Is a family concerned about a book you are reading or a lesson you are teaching? Find out the specifics of why. If it's part of a curriculum or program the school or district has asked you to use with students, families can address the curriculum coordinator about this issue. If it's not part of the curriculum or a program, share the norms of the class with families. Explain how you teach students to communicate about difficult and challenging topics with one another. Let them know the conversation isn't a free-for-all, but rather that, as a professional educator, you guide students to discuss relevant and challenging topics with care and guidance, in a developmentally appropriate way. If they still disagree, that is okay! You can still do what you think is best and most inclusive for your students, and if you are unsure, you can run it by your teaching team or your principal.

If you live in a place where language related to diversity is being challenged, consider how you can affirm your students' identities and teach factual histories while also protecting yourself from any disciplinary action. Stay in touch with teacher leaders and union representatives in your school to understand how they are handling these issues. You want to create an inclusive and safe class community and you also want to keep your job. In our country right now, this is a big challenge. Focus on your locus of control, work to protect and affirm students, and find your allies and community to support you.

Dig Deeper

- **Read** This teacher panel on high impact parent engagement: a website with many family interaction tools. https://www.familyengagementlab.org/blog-archive/teacher-panel-shares-strategies-for-advancing-student-success-through-family-engagement
- **Review** Engaging Families and Caregivers guide from Learning for Justice.
- **View** *4 Ways to Support Partnerships with Families* in Edutopia. https://www.edutopia.org/article/building-strong-relationships-parents/

- **Consider** This example survey for families for PreK: NYC Department of Education resource with ideas for how to get to know families, including an example survey. https://infohub.nyced.org/docs/default-source/default-document-library/beginning-of-year-questionnaire-for-families-english.pdf
- **Review** Another example, this one from Pernille Ripp: http://bit.ly/3ORBEqX
- **View** This student-led conference resource list from Edutopia: https://www.edutopia.org/blog/student-led-conferences-resources-ashley-cronin

 ### Reflect, Dream, Plan

- Which ways to connect with families resonate with you?
- Which might stretch you a bit, but feel good after you've done them?

Build Your Playlist

> What song about families might be a good pick for your playlist?
>
>

Identify Your Big Three

What are the Big Three ways you will connect with families this year? What actions will you take?

1.

2.

3.

8

Leading a Busy Classroom

Chapter Overview

You may be wondering how you will establish a classroom of respect, collaboration, and structure that allows everyone to thrive. This will happen as you gain experience and learn what works (and what doesn't) in how you manage your own classroom. But we hope to shorten that learning curve a bit. This chapter will offer many of the tools and ideas we have generated from experience and research, identify several great resources, and – as always – feature thoughts from experienced teachers.

> Don't take student behavior personally. Kids are traveling their own rocky road in life and doing the best they can. Remember that behavior is just communication, and they are often seeking connection.
> —Julie Smart, Special Educator

Connect

It was Katy's second teaching position, and the school was in rural Vermont. Katy had lovingly set up her classroom over the summer, including a big stuffed elephant her dad had bought her when she was a child. The elephant's name was Fred. His cozy presence created the perfect reading nook in the classroom library. Katy had saved a giant orange fish from a student who could no longer care for it, and it was swimming back and forth in a donated aquarium at the back of the room. She was so excited to share this space with students.

On the first day of school, the combined class of raucous fifth and sixth grade students looked surprised when Katy invited them to sit in a circle on the floor to begin the morning meeting. When they finally gathered and sat in a circle, they eagerly told her about the teacher she was taking over for. While constantly interrupting each other, they explained that they hated (!) him. That he'd yelled at them. And that when he'd fallen off his desk (sitting on the edge, as teachers sometimes do) one day, they'd laughed and laughed. During this retelling, one student left and sat under his desk.

Katy was shocked at the level of animus they felt for the teacher. She was also surprised at their lack of skills in meeting respectfully as a group. It's no surprise, then, that none of the day's teaching plans went as planned. The students were not accustomed to a climate where there were clear expectations, where students supported each other, and where they didn't just try to make the teacher mad. This had clearly been their project for the last year. Although the students didn't see, Katy left that day in tears. She knew she had her work cut out for her in creating a strong community from scratch, one based on respect, trust, collaboration, empathy, and kindness.

That night, Katy made a simple list of expectations for the class and what would happen if they weren't followed. You'll have read that making class norms and rules with the class is the way to go, and we agree. Getting students' buy in and ideas about how they want the class to be is essential. But this class needed a whole lot of structure, immediately, and consistency, immediately. So Katy created this for them, then worked back into student choice, voice, and community building once they were on track.

Katy also had to keep her emotions in check. After that first night of tears, she returned and was consistently calm, kind, and focused on the expectations of the class. She followed through with some breaks, one-on-one plans, and conferences. It took a few months of consistency, but the class got on track and the community was strong. The students learned their teacher wasn't going to shame, blame, or yell. They learned that they were safe and they could focus on learning. It wasn't easy, but it was necessary. They ended up having a great year together.

Real Talk

> Everyone says to try to remember that it isn't really about you, and that's true but can also be hard in the moment. So, it's also okay to tap out when you feel your own emotions getting the better of you. And it's okay if sometimes you lose your cool – we have all been there – but go back and APOLOGIZE. Sometimes those apologies are the best relationship-

> builder there are, because guess what? Those kids who sometimes lose it often carry a lot of secret embarrassment and shame about their behavior, and to see that adults own and apologize for their behavior goes a long way in helping to build respect, safety, and even their own self-reflection.
> —Triston Upson, Middle School English Language Arts teacher

Twenty years ago, this chapter would have been called "classroom management" or "managing student behavior." Writing a student's name on the board when they "misbehaved" or posting a public-facing behavior chart was common practice. Some names had gold stars, and some had none. Maybe some of you even experienced this as learners. We're very glad that the field of education has evolved, moving away from tactics that would cause needless shame or embarrassment to a more humane way of holding students accountable for their actions while honoring their dignity.

To be sure, leading our busy classrooms remains challenging. We can all fall back on old practices. Peter Lortie long ago coined the term "apprenticeship of observation" to describe the idea that we are each likely to teach the way we ourselves were taught (1975). We were apprentices to teaching by virtue of our role as learners. It's easy to fall back on practices, climates, and cultures we ourselves experienced as students in schools. But let's explore how to set you and your students up for success, so that we continue to progress rather than regress!

The first six weeks.

Those first six weeks of school are different from all the rest. This is the time to set the stage for the year. To build relationships. Routines. Structure. To build a strong community. To set norms and expectations. To develop teamwork and collaboration. These are essential for the functioning of a classroom.

If you work with younger students, you might have experience with Responsive Classroom, which focuses on the importance of the first six weeks of school in an intentional way. We think this is a great way to go, and direct you to their many resources for starting the school year off well at ResponsiveClassroom.org. We highlight several practices below, but encourage you to visit Responsive Classroom for more information on them.

> Be consistent and follow through! There's a lot about the "first six weeks" and learning rules and routines, and yes, that's crucial. But be sure that there's something curricular that grabs them right away. Take a walk in

> late summer/early fall weather and notice things. Tie it into a book. Read a chapter from a funny but powerful book every day – don't skip it. Humor/laughing together pulls a group into a community and becomes a ritual. And yes, model, role play, and calmly follow through on the routines and norms that will see you through the year.
> —Valerie Bang-Jensen, Professor of Education Emerita

Norms, Norms, Norms

No matter the age of your students, the structure of your classroom, or the schedule of your classes, setting norms through a collaborative process is essential. Norms are shared agreements for how to be together. They set the tone of a class, provide clear behavioral guidelines, decrease instances of incivility, and enable students and teachers to feel safe expressing their ideas and viewpoints (Cornell Center for Teaching Innovation, n.d.). Indeed, norms are the very foundation of a safe place for dialogue and learning.

Collaborate with students in developing your classroom norms. In a circle, ask the students how they want the classroom to feel this year. What do they hope to accomplish? What kind of climate will help them get there? What conditions will help them learn the most this year? How can they make this happen? Invite them to brainstorm with a partner what kinds of norms or guidelines are needed to help them meet these goals. Then pair the partners with another set of partners, creating a group of four. Ask them to combine their ideas. Continue the process of prioritizing and revising until the full class decides on a short list of norms. We have found between three and six norms is usually right on. Then print or write these up in color, and hang them in a prominent place in the classroom. Invite students – and even families – to sign and return them to show agreement and consensus. Students will have ownership of this process if they help to derive these themselves.

We suggest you revisit the norms often, asking questions like "How are we doing with these?" "What might we want to add or change?" "How does it feel here?" "What might we need to work on?" Revisiting them often reminds the class that everyone is an important part of making the community function. Norms are the building blocks of creating a safe, warm, and supportive community that holds everyone accountable for their behavior and actions. It also models what a strong, democratic community can look like.

How do we want to be? (Figure 8.1).

It's worth asking students how they want to BE this academic year, and thinking of a word to describe it. Katy often made a bulletin board in

Figure 8.1 Photo of How to BE.

the classroom out of these commitments. Students would write their word commitments and aspirations for how they wanted to BE (like "accepting," "brave," "kind," and "organized") on long pieces of posterboard. The bulletin board was centrally located in the classroom and they reflected on it regularly. They would consider, How were we today? Which one did you want to work on tomorrow?

Team Building for the Win!

Strong and healthy communities are intentionally built. From the first day of school, leading students in ice-breakers or community-building activities does several things. It helps students get to know each other, builds teamwork skills, and fosters a sense of belonging and joy. You can do so with limited materials and space, in the classroom or outside. Luckily, there are lots of great team-building activities out there, so this is one place where you definitely don't need to reinvent the wheel!

Some classics include:

- Marshmallow Challenge: Students work together to build the tallest freestanding tower of marshmallows by using only the materials given to them. These can include 20 pieces of pasta, one yard of string, one yard of masking tape, and marshmallows!
- Pass the Can: Materials needed: large coffee-type can. Have your class sit in a circle on the floor with their feet pointed into the center. The challenge is for students to pass the can around the circle, without it touching the ground or using their hands or upper bodies. If it touches the ground, the group must start again. The can has to go over everyone's foot at least once.
- Hula Hoop Circles: Materials needed: hula hoop. Have your class stand in a circle and put the hula hoop through on the student's arm. Have the students hold hands in the circle, and tell them they must not break the circle. They must pass it around the circle without breaking their contact with the other students, so each student will need help passing the hula hoop over their heads and bodies. Start again if a student drops the hand holding, and cheer for each other!
- Birthday Line Up: There are many versions of this one, but the main challenge is for students to line up silently by the date they were born. They will need to rely on nonverbal forms of communication. Allow for laughter!

You'll develop your favorites as time goes on, and a quick web search of these activities will yield others to try. They are worth the time. Your students need to learn how to work together, and they need these experiences.

You can also build community by helping students get to know each other. During the first six weeks of school, leading students in activities that showcase and validate who they are and their backgrounds is a beautiful way to foster their sense of belonging. Invite students to draw a self-portrait or take a selfie in a place or surrounded items that convey who they are. Ask them to make a "map of the self" that illustrates important places and features of their identity. Make time for them to share these and hang them up around the classroom.

> Teach your students executive functioning skills that support you as well as them. Clear agendas, organization of materials, time to clean cubbies, building routines that structure your time together as one where community is built, learning happens and time to tidy up and close up a lesson, take the time to teach transitions, they will help everyone. This is a hard job but you can do it! It is rewarding emotionally, socially, and academically. It is a community service and you become a part of the community in the school and beyond. We need your energy, expertise and enthusiasm to strive to create powerful experiences for students.
> —Vasanthi Meyette, Fifth and Sixth Science Teacher

Routines!

> Set routines and procedures early in the year. If kids know what is expected of them at the start of a class, for example, they get right down to it. With the kids knowing that when they walk into the room the first thing they do is grab their assignment books and jot down the homework and then they head to a comfortable reading spot and read for 15 minutes, it frees the teacher up to check in with individual kids.
> —Heidi Ringer, Librarian and former Fifth and Sixth Grade Teacher

A student's morning journey to your classroom can be wildly unpredictable, whether it's the bus, hallways, cafeteria, or wherever they spend time prior to arriving at your classroom door. These spaces can be daunting. When students get to your room, however, you have a chance to offer the structure that can put them at ease. Most students – in fact most humans! – benefit from knowing what to expect.

How will students know the daily or class schedule? Consider always posting the schedule of the day or class. This might go on your white board with the date at the top. Those students who crave predictability will review this carefully, and they will mentally prepare for the day.

How will students transition from one thing to the next? It's important for students to learn how to successfully transition from one class to another, or to lunch, recess, and home. Clear routines help students of all ages transition more successfully. Responsive Classroom does a nice job of developing a process for releasing responsibility for using different parts of the classroom and routines for transitions. Some teachers play certain music for transitions, some ring a chime, and others sing a clean-up song. For older students, play a popular song and challenge students to clean up before the song ends. Whatever you do, try not to involve much of your voice. You will get tired of reminding and talking your way through transitions, so if your students can understand expectations (where do the markers go?) and the process for lining up ultimately independently, you will save your voice and mindset. For older students, have a set procedure for cleaning up where students know their roles and the expectations.

How do students know where things go? All parts of the room deserve a discussion and process for use. These might include spaces for outdoor gear (where do wet coats and jackets go?), a classroom library or reading area (where can we sit? how do we check out books?), or the laptop rack (how do we put computers away? how do we charge them?). Flexible seating can be an especially important place to establish clear routines and expectations. One of our favorite classrooms had a big purple bathtub filled with pillows. Students loved to sit there to read. We are big fans of flexible seating. Students often sit and move in unique and different ways. Bean bags, yoga balls, low desks, stand up desks, desk bicycles, all provide students with varied ways to be and work in your classroom. In all cases, students can be set up for greater success when they understand the expectations for these seats, just like any classroom tool or space.

The first six weeks are the time to introduce these routines and reinforce them.

Understanding how the schedule and general classroom runs offers students a calm, structured environment. Of course there will be fire drills, spontaneous teachable moments, classes that run long, and the rest. But students will feel supported by having a basic structure in place. This will not happen overnight. Students, especially younger ones, will need time to learn and practice the routine. Rest assured, it's worth the time and will pay you back in the (mostly) smooth functioning of the class.

Each day is a new day. This is good for us as adults and it's good for the learners in our care. As the teacher, you may be holding on to something you did or didn't do the day before. Maybe you said something you wished you hadn't and you've been replaying it in your mind. Don't worry. Today is a new day. Begin afresh. It is also a new day for the students. Did one of them have a hard time yesterday? Give them the gift of a clean slate. Tell them that

> **PERMISSION SLIP**
>
> YOU ARE HEREBY GRANTED PERMISSION TO:
> - <u>SLOW DOWN</u> THE PROCESS OF REVIEWING EXPECTATIONS, ROUTINES, AND STRUCTURES
> - <u>SPEND THE TIME YOU NEED</u> ON THESE IMPORTANT FACETS OF YOUR COMMUNITY

you're glad they are here and that you're looking forward to working with them today. This way they know that you're not harboring negative feelings about what happened the day before. They have permission to begin anew. This will show that you are a reflective and compassionate teacher. For students who don't experience this regularly, it can be revolutionary.

Unconditional Positive Regard
Think back to your time as a student in elementary, middle or high school. Imagine if your teachers had offered you a fresh start every day! Unconditional Positive Regard is one of several stances we have found helpful in maintaining this revolutionary thinking. Coined by Carl Rogers (1951), and discussed by Alex Shevrin Venet (2023), the concept of Unconditional Positive Regard is exactly what it sounds like. It essentially means I care about you and nothing you do that will change that. My care for you is unconditional. You don't have to earn it. You don't have to have everything together for me to care about you. You are worthy of care, support, and love just by being in this class. By being part of our community.

This is an essential mindset for teachers. And, to be sure, there are times when this can be hard. That's okay. You can process your feelings with a mentor, friend, or the principal. You can reflect while spending time in nature, resting, or at home. But each day, remember that your job is to care for these people. You're trying to make sure they have what they need to be successful. Each of your students deserves your positive regard, no matter what has happened or will happen. It is a radical and loving stance, and many students will push you, thinking that you can't possibly care for them if they never do homework, can't sit still, or follow directions. You have a huge chance to make an impact on these students, because you'll remember that this is a both-and profession. You can *both* offer unconditional positive regard *and* teach them safe boundaries. You can *both* care for them *and* teach them alternative choices.

Everyone Gets What They Need to Succeed

Effective classrooms are those in which everyone gets what they need to succeed. In these classrooms, different learners have different experiences and supports. One student leaves at the end of the day for one-on-one time with a behavior specialist, another student has extended time for assessments, and still another listens to an audio book instead of visually reading it. Students get what they need in order to succeed. This is the essential difference between "equal" (everyone gets the same thing) and equitable (everyone gets what they need, knowing they are starting from different places). This focus on equitable learning opportunities is an essential element of culturally responsive practice. Developed by Gloria Ladson-Billings (1995), culturally responsive practice puts students' belonging, identity, and lived experiences at the center of the classroom practices. It "uses students' customs, characteristics, experiences, and perspectives as tools for better classroom instruction (Will & Najarro, 2023)." According to Geneva Gay, "when academic knowledge and skills are situated within the lived experiences and frames of reference for students, they are more personally meaningful, have higher interest appeal, and are learned more easily and thoroughly (2018, p. 106)." In culturally responsive classrooms, students, especially those from historically marginalized groups, are valued for who they are. They are seen for their assets and not their deficits. Similarly, including representation of historically marginalized populations, from scientists, mathematicians, writers, and artists, shows students they can be it if they SEE it. This is a teacher boost too – watching your students see their own potential rise is a sure-fire mood booster and motivator.

Meeting Students' Basic Needs

By now you've probably heard the phrase "Maslow before Bloom." Maslow's Hierarchy of Needs (1943) asserted that students' physiological needs for food, water, shelter, clothing, and sleep were essential precursors to the kind of academic learning represented in Bloom's Taxonomy (1956). Indeed, there's ample research to support this idea. Students must have their basic needs met in order to learn.

While we are encouraged by the increase in "community schools" (Maier et al., 2017), in which students can access food, dental and medical care, unfortunately too many students still come to school hungry, tired, or even hurting. Often, teachers can think a student is "misbehaving" when they're simply hungry. You can do some basic things to help. Allow water bottles in the classroom, for one (and provide them if needed). Have a snack drawer that students can access. Know ahead of time where your school nurse (or counselor or social worker or principal) keeps extra clothes and shoes. To be clear, we don't want you paying out of your pocket for these things; we know too many teachers who do. These items are often supplied by donations from the parent teacher organization.

Culture of Caring

It is up to us to create a culture of caring in the classroom. Even in a divided world, we can create an environment that is rooted in community, safety, equity, and caring. There are lots of ways to do this, but modeling calm, care, listening, and power-sharing all help. There are lots of intentional practices in this area as well.

For example, think about how the day starts and ends. In the morning, it can be hard to jump from a home and/or bus environment into a school day. Students may need a moment. At the start of a class, or the day, can they arrive and take a few minutes to read, draw, say hi to a neighbor, and settle in? We need to start learning, of course, but this soft start can yield more learning precisely because students have settled in. This can look like ten minutes with music playing, students quietly chatting or drawing, or watching a wildlife camera on the Smartboard, before assembling as a whole group. It can also be helpful to think about the end of the day. Closing meetings are great for this! Gather students in a circle and read dismissal notes. Then ask them an end of the day question. What went well today? Who can you shout out to and why? What is an aha, apology, or appreciation you can offer about the day? Students will leave on this positive note.

Manage Your Emotions and Reactions

> Create mantras for yourself that you can use before, after, and during classes. My favorites are "it's not personal," "these are children," and "I don't know what they are going through."
> —Life LeGeros, Civics and Equity Teacher

We've talked about this in Chapter 3 but it is worth mentioning again here. None of this will work if you are not managing your emotions as a teacher. Nothing breaks a community as much as yelling, shaming, or belittling students or others. It can be hard, but try to take a pause before reacting to challenging behavior. Take a breath, and then reflect. Does the student need a different seat, a break, or a one-on-one talk? Use a calm but direct voice, and get on the students' eye level if possible. Reacting without thinking can damage the classroom community. Remember, you are the leader, and the students are watching to see how you will react and will base their future decisions on this.

Normalize pausing and reflecting. It is okay to pause, take breaks, and circle back! You can say to students, "Whew! I need a minute to think about this. Don't worry, we will circle back to this tomorrow. Let's all have a think about what happened and come in tomorrow ready to talk about it."

> Be okay with a pause, with no words. Just pause, think, react.
> —Honi Bean Barrett, Fifth and Sixth Grade Teacher

Find Your Delights

Ross Gay, poet and writer, advises his readers to look for "delights" each day (2019). He suggests that, as you begin to look, you will notice more of them

> It can be easy to focus only on the challenges you faced in a day or the things you wish you had handled differently and this can undermine your confidence and enjoyment of teaching. When I found myself focusing too much on the negative, I would write those things down so I wouldn't continue to ruminate on them but then I would also write about some positives and things I did well during the day. It is important to cultivate a practice of focusing on your successes.
> —High School Social Studies Teacher

and take joy from that. We suggest it is the same with teaching. As you fall asleep at night, think, what went well today? What was silly, fun, or even just successful? Make that mental list in your head, or, better yet, write it down! This will lead to better sleep, for one, and remind you that you are making progress each day.

In schools, there will always be negative things to focus on. These big systems often have many problems. You could spend every teaching day of your life focused on these problems. And there are many. The more you focus on them, the more you will notice. You can also find people to admire the problems with. They are everywhere. But this will quickly exhaust you. While we want to avoid being toxically positive (everything is GREAT! forced smile!), it *is* helpful to try and make change where you can, and solve both small and large problems, all while trying to maintain a positive mindset. Sure, it's hard and you won't achieve it every day. With all the challenges in public schools, it can seem especially insurmountable. But you entered this extraordinary profession with a value, a passion, and a motivation to make a difference, and you are doing it. So find people who lift you up, help you solve problems, and support your forward momentum. **Adopt a spirit of realistic optimism**. The work you do matters and is worthy. Try again each day. Then rest, reflect, and rejuvenate. Rinse and repeat. That's all we can do!

Dig Deeper

- **Read** *43 Awesome Teambuilding Activities for Kids* from We Are Teachers: https://www.weareteachers.com/team-building-games-and-activities/
- **Review** *17 Fun Teambuilding Activities for Kids in Your Classroom* from Prodigy https://www.prodigygame.com/main-en/blog/team-building-activities-for-kids/
- **Visit** https://gokidpower.org/fun-team-building-activities-for-kids/ to view *22 Fun Team Building Games & Activities for Kids* (note different age bands)

Reflect, Dream, Plan

- How will you build a strong community in your classroom?
- What ideas from this chapter are you thinking about trying to build collaboration and teamwork?
- When you picture your classroom, with all of your students in it thriving, what do you see?

Draw or write about your classroom here.

Build Your Playlist

> What song speaks to you about building community and having a positive experience with students?

Identify Your Big Three

Your turn! What are your top three actions from this chapter to promote a thriving and engaged class community you will focus on this school year?

1.

2.

3.

9
Pulling It All Together

> **Chapter Overview**
> Congratulations, you've made it this far. We hope this many-course meal at our dining table has been helpful to you, and that you've learned from these experienced teachers' stories and advice. You're joining a long line of people dedicated to the next generation, to raising educated, compassionate, caring students who will become (and already are) responsible, engaged, and critical thinking citizens of the world. This chapter will offer some final thoughts; some are lofty and some are tactical but all send you on your way with our very best wishes. Know you are not alone in this journey. The long dining table of generations of teachers is here for you, in books, online, down the hall, in community groups, and other collaborations.

> Just remember that there will be at least one young person who will make your day tomorrow and another for whom you are the reason they continue to enjoy learning.
>
> —@juliaerin80

Real Talk

> Teaching is both challenging and rewarding. Our students need you. Our communities need you. Our country needs you. Now more than ever. I like to think of starting a new job in groups of 3. First 3 weeks – listen, learn resources. First 3 months – understand your community, settle in for a bumpy ride. It's bumpy. There is a lot to learn. Give yourself grace. First 3 years – Through three years and you're rocking… you've got a handle of the curriculum, student needs, community needs, and are ready to showcase your own craft and creativity in your instruction. Enjoy!
>
> —Tim Mulligan, Principal

Teaching Is Developmental

Just as learning is developmental, so too is teaching. It's ok not to know everything all at once. Take a longer-term approach to build up steam as a teacher. Like Tim says, give yourself grace, and give yourself at least three years to be fully up and running and feeling good. You cannot expect to be an expert as a teacher at the beginning. It will take years to get your systems, mindset, tools, and plans up and running. And that is okay! Don't put too much pressure on yourself to know everything. This can be hard on the perfectionistic types, but the job of teaching is rooted in lifelong learning. Use every year, and even every day, as "an opportunity to continuously grow, learn, ask questions, be confused, and overcome challenges" (Willis, 2007, p. 8). This is a teacher-sustaining practice.

At first, work on learning as much as you can from others, both in your school and beyond. Work on developing a strong, respectful class community and building relationships with others in the building. As Maslow (1943) reminds us, we can't make progress with students unless they have their socio-emotional, physiological, safety, and belongingness needs met. So focus on developing your class community where students treat you and each other well (most of the time). Then start working on the curriculum. Focus on one area at a time to get up to speed. Work with coaches and your mentor in these areas and build up strength over time. It can also help to develop a curriculum map for the year, based on your standards, teaching team, grade level focus, and programs your school may expect you to use. Of course it will change based on conditions in your class, but it can provide a clear vision for the year and can be shared with parents and caregivers.

Language Matters

> How we talk about education matters. It becomes the soil in which our assumptions are rooted. We speak our beliefs in the descriptors and metaphors we select.
>
> —Sherri Spelic, 2017

The language we attach to concepts, ideas, and people impacts our perspectives on what we are describing. The words those around us use do as well. We often hear people use words like "in the trenches" to describe teaching. Or "heading into battle" for going into a school day, or being on the "battlefield" being the classroom. Consider how teachers are described as being on the "frontline" with students, as they help students and handle daily challenges and issues that emerge. While metaphors like this may at times feel accurate for the daily real life experiences of teachers, they don't help us create the world we want to see inside schools. Teachers are trying to work in a fractured society, and often in broken school systems. But your classroom is the opportunity to create a community where students learn and interact bravely and with compassion, where they develop curiosity and other skills that cultivate a shared humanity, and where civic responsibility exists. Teachers are often trying to create the world they want to see, one they believe in as possible. One way to do that is to flip the language and metaphors to be ones that promote peace, justice, and community instead. We appreciate Lindsey Halman and Pat LaClair's (ASCD, 2024) reversal of the war metaphor. They ask, "What if we asked our new teachers not to be 'boots on the ground,' but 'cultivators of community'?" Indeed, research has shown that "negative co-rumination" can be contagious. In fact, teachers who frequently talked about what was wrong with their school were more apt to demonstrate signs of burnout than those who had more positive conversations (ASCD, 2024).

We've both had times in our teaching careers when we had to work hard to maintain a positive mindset. For Katy, it was the effect of a powerful teacher clique that was fueled by negative talk about others. People were grumpy and fueled by grievances, complaints, and rumors. For Penny, it was the presence of a toxic teammate who was determined to bring everyone down with him, always finding reasons to put his own needs ahead of their shared students. In both cases, negative co-rumination was rampant in the building. This, in turn, increased our feelings of emotional exhaustion, which, as we've established, is a key component of burnout (Freudenberger, 1974; Maslach & Jackson, 1981).

> If you find the teachers' room in your school to be a negative place, avoid it at all costs. Nothing will bring you down faster than listening to others' complaints.
> —Marc Ducharme, High School Social Studies Teacher

Marc is right. Negativity can spread like a contagion. It's tricky that way. And anyone can fall into it. He's not suggesting you can simply avoid the problems at your school and pretend everything is okay, and nor are we. But we are suggesting that how we talk about our job matters. It impacts our mental health and our sustainability in the profession. And it affects those around us. Reframing language can be challenging, but even noticing our words, and not accepting the premise, is a good start.

Hope Is a Choice

> Teaching is the greatest act of optimism.
> —Colleen Wilcox

Hope is a daily choice, and a positive worldview. It is not Pollyannaism, but a belief in community and in other human beings. It can be challenging, for sure. But avoiding cynicism can have a dramatic impact on your wellness in and out of the classroom. Avoiding cynicism is a teacher-sustaining behavior, because cynicism is a key component of burnout. Research shows that feeling a strong sense of community with high trust between people is beneficial for physical and mental health (Vedantam, 2023). Teachers who adopt a cynical worldview, believing people to be untrustworthy, are not great teachers, at least in terms of their relationships to their students and their own health outcomes (Vedantam, 2023).

In contrast to cynicism, choosing hope offers great benefits. Hopeful people are more resilient when faced with difficulties (Murphy, 2023). Hope, like our muscles, needs to flex often to strengthen. Psychologist Jamil Zaki started putting his groundbreaking research on hope into practice. He said,

> *I try to notice positive things in my everyday life, and in particular, positive things that other people do. I actually started this as a practice with my kids because I realized I was griping to them about all sorts of people and maybe giving them a negative view of the world. So I started trying to notice for them and tell them about everyday positive acts that I had seen. And I noticed that this habit of action, of speech turned into a habit of mind. It was like*

> *knowing that I wanted to share positive stories with them popped an antenna out of my head and made me curious and hungry for evidence of positive and kind acts. And once that antenna popped up, it was not hard to find those acts. They are everywhere. It was like changing the lens through which I saw the social world and suddenly alerted me to a world full of generous and open minded and warm people.*
>
> (Vedantam, 2023)

Even on your worst days as a teacher, we bet you can think of a few positive things that happened. This is the work of holding on to hope.

Each day, when you wake up as a teacher, you have a choice. You can go into the day with the knowledge that you are making a difference in people's lives, and that what you do matters. You can carry forward with hope, that you believe in the next generation and are working to make our collective humanity more compassionate, knowledgeable, caring, and informed. On many days, this will feel hard. But focusing on hope while working in a challenging system can fill your life with purpose and focus. And that might be the best medicine for a good life, as long as you balance that sense of obligation with a similar commitment to take care of yourself. It is a delicate balance to be sure. But with these practices, and your long dining table of fellow educators supporting you, hope is a great option.

Be Ready for Change

We know it might be hard to imagine. Right now, you're doing your job, day in and day out. Trying to be healthy. Doing your best for your students. But you never know what is coming next, or what might change for you. The only thing we know is our world, and our current situations, is always changing. The only constant is change. Maybe your district administrators (hopefully with your input!) decide your expertise is needed at another grade level or in another school building. Maybe you'll have taken family leave and need to get back into the profession. Perhaps you earn an additional teaching endorsement. You might find that your school is not the right fit for you anymore. Maybe you just like keeping your options open, feeling in charge of your destiny. For whatever reason, conditions and expectations change. To prepare for this change – planned or unplanned – we suggest you keep good documentation of all of your great work, ideas, and progress as an educator. Here are a few ways to be ready for *whatever* comes your way, *whenever* it does.

First, be sure to back up your curricular creations and plans. Over the course of your career, you will create many wonderful lessons, units, and assessments. You'll likely store them on your school's Google Domain or on another shared drive. These materials are invaluable. You'll use them regularly and you might not think about future access. We're here to tell you that these are important parts of your teaching history. Once you leave, it's unlikely that you will be able to retrieve anything you created. If everything lives on the school's domain, you'll lose access to your emails, your calendar, your docs, your slide shows, and your forms.

We suggest you download these things every year. Use Google TakeOut or another backup system. Make sure you have a copy of all that you have created. If you make it a regular practice, you will have an organized set of materials backed up and ready. Similarly, take pictures of projects, bulletin boards, and your classroom setup. This takes little time but comes in handy as a reference if you move schools, or need to supply a portfolio of your work for recertification, or to get into a graduate school.

Second, document your professional development. Have you ever searched your drives or even past computers for something you wrote or received years ago? Spending your one precious life searching for something you are pretty sure exists but you have no idea where? Create a folder on your desktop or in your personal Google Drive, Drop Box, or whatever archive you use. Label it something like *Evidence of Professional Development*. No seriously. Do it right now. Put the book down and open your laptop. Then, each time you participate in any form of professional development or training, download the documentation of your participation into this folder. And don't forget to include that professional development on your resume.

And speaking of resumes... Keep yours current. The simple trick to keeping your resume up-to-date is to continually add to it. Did you participate in a recent training? Include it on your resume. Attend a conference? Add it. Finish a micro credential or a badge? Write it down. Serve as advisor for a new student organization? You guessed it, add it to your resume. If you develop this habit, you can avoid the enormous task of updating your resume when you may need it quickly and/or during a stressful time. An added bonus is that it feels good to see the growth! You're doing lots of things, they are valuable, and now they're documented.

Remember Your Values

> Trust yourself and stay true to your belief system. All kids can learn!
> —Special Educator

Remembering why you went into teaching, and what your values are can be a challenge in day-to-day teaching. When you are doing bus duty, making groups during lunch, or answering emails, it can be easy to forget why you are doing this job. Elena Aguilar (2018) has written extensively about how to sustain and thrive as a teacher. She reminds us that our values are a guiding light for us, especially in challenging times. Aguilar outlines a process for identifying your values and sharing them with other educators. This values list and process is free and available in our Dig Deeper section of this chapter. Even the simple act of reflecting, narrowing, and identifying a few core values is motivating. Consider doing this with your teacher team, to both reflect individually and then share to build community and knowledge about where your teammates are coming from. Write them down and post them near your desk. Keep them on your phone. Put them anywhere you have easy access so you can remind yourself why you do this crucial work.

> On your worst days, you'll feel like you don't belong in the profession and that you are doing your students a disservice. On your best days, you'll feel like you're making a real difference. Let all the feelings wash over you. You are a learner, too. You are growing, too.
> —Fourth Grade Teacher

We know you lead a busy teaching life and you don't need more to do. But we promise, identifying your values can be motivating and clarifying. They can help guide you when things are tough. They can remind you why you are doing this. Maybe you like to journal. This can be particularly helpful before going to sleep because it can empty your mind of your worries and thoughts before you rest. Even if you don't write it down, reflection like this is useful. Quintanilla (2023) offers prompts for teachers to focus on values. Questions like "What moments of joy or connection reaffirmed my values today?" and "Where did I deviate from my values today, and how can I realign myself tomorrow?" and "How did my values influence my decisions in today's challenges?" can help us see where we are living our values, where we might be deviating from them, and how to try again tomorrow. Consider one of these questions as a thought exercise tomorrow, maybe while commuting or walking the dog.

We have discussed noting delights or joys from each day teaching as a regular gratitude practice earlier in the book. One way you can tailor this around your values is to focus on what happened that day (decisions you made, activities you led, conversations you had) that reflected your values. Over time, it becomes a habit, and you increase your self-awareness.

Quintanilla (2023) also suggests daily affirmations. These are statements you can craft based on your identified values. This might sound a little woo-woo for some of you, but a guiding statement can be illuminating and clarifying, especially when you are dealing with the minutiae of teaching! It can be something simple such as "Today I am guided by ..." or "I will teach with ..." or "I believe in...." These simple statements can guide you, focus you on what matters, and give you clarity in an often confusing and overwhelming world.

Remember Your Impact

> A teacher affects eternity; he can never tell where his influence stops.
> —Henry Adams

You are the leader of the learning environment. Remember that you set the tone for the classroom. If you come in stressed and rushing around, the students will mimic, or in some other way react to, that vibe. If you come in calm, friendly, and focused, they will similarly mimic that tone, and their nervous systems will be more likely to regulate. You may think you have little control as a new teacher. Or you might believe that your impact is limited. On the contrary, while you may not have control over the curriculum you are expected to follow, you have a great deal of control about many, many things as a teacher. You are the reason they enjoy learning, they come to school, they feel safe, they feel a sense of belonging, they understand something new, they make a connection, they feel seen.

You are the creator of access. You attend to your students' needs and learning. You are the one who notices if a student needs food, or help with hygiene, or a safety check. This is powerful. You change the course of a life with these actions. Every day. Each year. While that can be scary, it is also empowering. You matter. Your showing up and doing your best for them matters. You can sleep well at night and know you are having a positive impact on the lives and worlds of your students, and the ripple effect on families and communities reverberates for the rest of their lives. In many ways, you will never know the impact of your work. It could take hold years later, in subtle and not so subtle ways.

> I've come to a frightening conclusion that I am the decisive element in the classroom. It's my personal approach that creates the climate. It's my daily mood that makes the weather. As a teacher, I possess a tremendous power to make a child's life miserable or joyous. I can be a tool of torture or an instrument of inspiration. I can humiliate or heal. In all situations, it is my response that decides whether a crisis will be escalated or de-escalated and a child humanized or dehumanized.
> —Haim Ginott

This Haim Ginott quote took Katy's breath away the first time she read it. It was in an educational magazine (yes, people used to read hard copy magazines!) and she ripped it out and hung it on her bulletin board near her desk. It can be hard to remember, when you're assessing papers and rushing to the next meeting, but how teachers show up for students, moment to moment, matters. It can have a huge impact on them.

> You are doing such an important job – hang in there. It's incredible that we expect novice teachers to do the same job as someone who has been teaching for years; it's a steep learning curve. But you were hired – you have something the school wants! Bring your energy and newest teaching strategies (great new books, new approaches, new experiences) to your team. They will learn as much from you as you do from them.
> —Valerie Bang-Jensen, Professor of Education Emerita

Dig Deeper

- **Read** Edutopia: *4 Practices that Help Teachers Navigate Change*. https://www.edutopia.org/article/maintaining-your-core-values-teacher/
- **Visit** ASCD: *Leading from your Core Values*. https://ascd.org/el/articles/leading-from-your-core-values
- **Identify** your core values with Elena Aguilar's free resources found at https://www.onwardthebook.com.

Reflect, Dream, Plan

- How will you avoid the co-rumination spiral?
- Where will you keep your personal archive of teaching materials?
- How will you get ready for your next opportunity, a little bit at a time? Draw or list some ideas here.

Build Your Playlist

What songs help you pull it all together and get moving?

Now you have your personalized playlist to help you remember your goals and dreams for sustaining a healthy, happy career in education!

Identify Your Big Three

Read over Your Big Three from previous chapters. Consider, which are you most excited about? Which will be most important? Most challenging to do? Identify those that will most help you be the person you want to be. Return to them often.

1.

2.

3.

Welcome to this incredibly powerful, dynamic, engaging, and challenging field. We are SO glad you are here. You can do this. Develop your systems of support. Take good care of your students and yourself. **We believe in you**.

CAUTION
Only read on if you feel ready for the next step
(and perhaps you have slept recently!)

Afterword: Becoming a Teacher Leader

You thought it was over, but no! You know how sometimes, when you watch all of the credits at the end of the movie, there's just a little bit more that is unexpected?

Here's your little bit more.

This book has offered some of the basic information for starting and maintaining a positive, healthy, and happy first few years of teaching. We know it isn't easy and that you'll have your own specific learning curve. The first three to five years of teaching are about learning how to do the job, and how to manage your life, with all of its emotions and demands. If you can do the first 5 years, you can absolutely do 20, 30, or more. You are well on your way.

But you might also be wondering what is next for you, after you learn the ropes and start to hit your stride with the job. While teaching doesn't have as explicit a career ladder as many other fields do, there are lots of ways to lean into your interests, develop leadership and specialized skills, and embrace opportunities that are professionally challenging and sustaining. It's all about navigating in directions that feel right to you. Here we discuss just a few of those many possible directions.

Assume Leadership Positions

Teaching is a natural place to develop leadership skills. Every day, you work with somewhere between 20 and 125 students, maybe less, maybe more. You're leading them in a year of learning. You are constantly managing this project, reflecting, and adjusting in real time. This is a perfect place to develop your leadership skills. Similarly, when meeting with your teacher team, you learn how to negotiate, develop agendas, assume different roles, and complete specific tasks. These are invaluable skills that you pick up just from doing the job and working collaboratively. Take advantage of this learning. Notice how coaches, other teachers, or special educators lead the meetings. How do they do it when it is effective, and what is happening when it is not effective? Reflect on this and build these skills. As you become more experienced, you can start exercising more leadership, be it in committees or in your teaching team. Join the committees you are passionate about and have some time for. Don't overcommit (as we talked about in the boundaries chapter). Keep practicing and learning. Make time for the work that both fuels and challenges you.

Develop Specialized Expertise

Most teachers we know have become experts at a particular area of professional interest. Some have pursued a deep place-based focus, having developing an integrated unit of study that is the hallmark of the academic year. They are regularly invited to talk to others about this signature unit, and generations of students and families look forward to it. Others have become experts in creating a student-centered learning environment, integrating a high degree of differentiation and flexible seating. These teachers write about these innovations, invite others to observe, and even do action research on these learning environments. Still others have become skilled math or literacy coaches or interventionists, working in targeted ways with learners and teachers.

Some teachers lead by getting involved in community or political organizations, and some start writing for educational outlets. In most cases, these folks have jumped into professional development that grows and stretches them in different ways, including through graduate courses, certificate programs, master's or doctoral degrees, or additional certifications. Additional degrees and coursework can help most teachers move up on the salary scale and help challenge you, grow your skills, expand your perspectives, and, eventually, open doors for new possibilities in the field of education.

Research What Works

Some educators choose to engage in action research, by implementing an innovation in their classroom and collecting data about the impact on students' experience. There are lots of great resources and graduate courses out there that can help you with this. Start with a researchable question and progress to an action research plan, where you write about the planned innovation in detail. Consider how you will collect student data (interview, observations, document reviews, focus groups?). Better yet, engage students themselves in defining the question and collecting and analyzing the data! If you get bit by the research bug, consider connecting with your local college or university to learn more about how to understand and conduct educational research.

Either way, be sure to share what you're learning with your teaching team and principal, with others at local or state conferences, or in education publications.

Share Your Work

Speaking of sharing your work! There are a wide variety of conferences held each year for teachers. So many it can be overwhelming. But fear not, they are here for you, based on your interests. Some will be very expensive, and it often makes sense to join the professional organization associated with the conference, which brings down the cost. Sometimes schools will cover this membership fee, and you can apply for funding to attend the conference. These are good opportunities to build a wider community of professionals interested in similar curriculum, grade levels, or issues. To start, attend one or two a year and consider which one you want to keep up with. See what feels good and where you find a community of shared interest where you get a lot out of the work. Then, when you're ready to present your innovative practice or action research project, you're already familiar with the conference. Submitting a proposal to present is a good challenge, a fabulous learning experience, a chance to grow your presentation skills, and an opportunity to gain professional visibility.

You might also want to start writing about education for media outlets. We love Edutopia, which is a super useful website that accepts posts from teachers across the country. We post there when we can, and use their posts within our courses with pre-service teachers. Many other blogs, such as We Are Teachers and Ed Week, also offer creative and fulfilling outlets.

Advocate for Change

As a teacher you have a front row seat in how public education works (and often doesn't). You are in a crucial position to advocate for change at the local, state, and national levels. For one, you can engage in policy development that can make a big impact in your school. Get on the district committees where policies are made where you can use your voice and experience. Your work could be in developing a clear vision for the school or in how book challenges will be handled. Or it could be in promoting the district's support for providing a free breakfast to all students (what a huge positive impact!). You can also join your teachers' union and support public education in your state and in the nation. Public schools are often under threat; if you believe in what public education has to offer, this might be another good avenue of leadership and advocacy. Your state legislature is also another avenue for advocacy. They take on issues relating to public education regularly, and your voice on budgeting, safety, curriculum can be an important perspective that is often overlooked. We have both testified on various issues at our state house over the years. These are incredible opportunities to share your knowledge and experience with politicians who have a direct hand in influencing public education. Whatever it is, find your passion and decide where you want to effect the most change.

All in all, your pathway is up to you. It might lead you to remain in the classroom and constantly evolve your teaching. It might lead you to another opportunity in education. But know this: You are needed in this field. Public education can give every kid a shot at success, and you, with your skills, your voice, and your leadership, play a key role in that success.

It's Really the End Now

So now you've *really* reached the end of this book. No more rolling end credits. Thank you for sharing time with us. Your efforts, your spirit, and your whole self in this impactful career are important to us. You matter, every day, to the health and opportunity of so many children and youth across our country. Your impact is beyond measure. We want you to thrive in this sometimes challenging and always changing profession. We hope this book has helped even if just a little bit.

Wishing you health, happiness, purpose, and a long satisfying career in education.

References

Aguilar, E. (2018). *Onward: Cultivating emotional resilience in educators.* John Wiley & Sons.

Alexander, C., Wyatt-Smith, C., & Du Plessis, A. (2020). The role of motivations and perceptions on the retention of inservice teachers. *Teaching and Teacher Education, 96*(103186). https://doi.org/10.1016/j.tate.2020.103186

Angelou, M. (1987). Interview with Oprah Winfrey on Super Soul Sunday. OWN Network.

Annenburg Classroom. (n.d.) *Civic education.* Retreived February 8, 2025 from https://www.annenbergclassroom.org/glossary_term/civic-education/

ASCD. (2024). Why do we use war metaphors to talk about teaching? Retrieved November 26, 2024, from https://ascd.org/blogs/why-do-we-use-war-metaphors-to-talk-about-teaching

Bishop, P. A., Downes, J. M., Netcoh, S., Farber, K., DeMink-Carthew, J., Brown, T., & Mark, R. (2020). Teacher roles in personalized learning environments. *The Elementary School Journal, 121*(2), 311–336.

Bloom, B. S. (Ed.). (1956). Taxonomy of educational objectives: The classification of educational goals. *Handbook I: Cognitive domain.* Longmans, Green.

Bray, B., & McClaskey, K. (2015). *Making learning personal.* Corwin Press.

Brown, B. (2015). *Rising strong: How the ability to reset transforms the way we live, love, parent, and lead.* Spiegel & Grau.

Brown, B. (2012). *Daring greatly: How the courage to be vulnerable transforms the way we live, love, parent, and lead.* Gotham Books.

Brown, B. (2010). *The gifts of imperfection.* Hazelden.

Brown, B. (2010). The power of vulnerability [Video]. TEDxHouston. https://www.ted.com/talks/brene_brown_the_power_of_vulnerability

Brown, B. (2006). Brené Brown on the 3 things you can do to stop a shame spiral. Oprah.com. https://www.oprah.com/oprahs-lifeclass/brene-brown-on-the-3-things-you-can-do-to-stop-a-shame-spiral-video

Cacioppo, S., Zhou, H., Monteleone, G., Majka, E. A., Quinn, K. A., Ball, A. B., Norman, G. J., Casely-Hayford, J., Björklund, C., Bergström, G., Lindqvist, P., & Kwak, L. (2022). What makes teachers stay? A cross-sectional exploration of the individual and contextual factors associated with teacher retention in Sweden. *Teaching and Teacher Education, 113* (103664). https://www.sciencedirect.com/science/article/pii/S0742051X2200035X

Collaborative for Academic, Social, and Emotional Learning (CASEL). (2023). CASEL framework: What is SEL? https://casel.org/fundamentals-of-sel/what-is-the-casel-framework/

Cornell Center for Teaching Innovation. (n.d.). Establishing community agreements and classroom norms. Cornell University. https://teaching.cornell.edu/resource/establishing-community-agreements-and-classroom-norms

Dewey, J. (1933). *How we think: A restatement of the relation of reflective thinking to the educative process.* D.C. Heath.

Doyle, G. (Host). (2023, April 23). Laziness does not exist with Devon Price. (303) In We Can Do Hard Things. Cadence13. https://momastery.com/blog/we-can-do-hard-things-ep-303/

Edmin, C. (2021). *Stem, steam, make, dream: Reimagining the culture of science, technology, engineering, and mathematics.* Math Solutions Publications.

Farber. (2018, June 2.). *STEAM time at Ottauquechee: What does it look like?* University of Vermont. https://tiie.w3.uvm.edu/blog/steam-time-at-ottauquechee/

Freudenberger, H. J. (1974). Staff burnout. *Journal of Social Issues, 30*(1), 159–165. https://doi.org/10.1111/j.1540-4560.1974.tb00706.x

Gay, G. (2018). *Culturally responsive teaching: Theory, research, and practice* (3rd ed.). Teachers College Press.

Gay, R. (2019). *The book of delights: Essays.* Algonquin Books.

Global Goals. (n.d.). *The 17 goals.* Global Goals. https://www.globalgoals.org/goals/

Gosner, S. (2023). How perfectionism holds new teachers back. *Edutopia,* April 28, 2023. https://www.edutopia.org/article/how-perfectionism-holds-new-teachers-back/

Hall, L. R. (2022). Rest isn't a reward for the work; it's part of the work: A timeline of this quote. Retrieved November 17, 2024, from https://leesareneehall.com/rest-isnt-a-reward-for-the-work-its-part-of-the-work-a-timeline-of-this-quote/

Healy, T. (2023). *15-minute focus: Regulation and co-regulation: Accessible neuroscience and connection strategies that bring calm into the classroom.* National Center for Youth Issues.

Hooks, B. (1994). *Teaching to transgress: Education as the practice of freedom.* Routledge.

Kaye, C. B., & Associates. (2002). *KIDS as planners: A guide to strengthening students, schools, and communities through service-learning.* Service-Learning Press.

Ladson-Billings, G. (1995). Toward a theory of culturally relevant pedagogy. *American Educational Research Journal, 32*(3), 465–491.

Leonore Annenberg Institute for Civics. (n.d.). Understanding democracy: A hip pocket guide—Civic education. *Annenberg Classroom.* https://www.annenbergclassroom.org/resource/understanding-democracy-hip-pocket-guide/civic-education/#:~:text=The%20second%20component%20of%20civic,to%20keep%20and%20improve%20it

Lorde, A. (2017). *A burst of light: And other essays*. Courier Dover Publications.

Lortie, D. C. (1975). *Schoolteacher: A sociological study*. University of Chicago Press.

Maier, A., Daniel, J., Oakes, J., & Lam, L. (2017). *Community schools as an effective school improvement strategy: A review of the evidence*. Learning Policy Institute.

Maslach, C. (1978). Job burn-out: How people cope. *Public Welfare, 36,* 56–58.

Maslach, C., & Jackson, S. E. (1981). The measurement of experienced burnout. *Journal of Occupational Behavior, 2*(2), 99–113. https://doi.org/10.1002/job.4030020205

Maslow, A. H. (1943). A theory of human motivation. *Psychological Review, 50*(4), 370–396.

Matuson, R. (2022, October 4). The attraction of subtraction: Why less means more productivity. *Forbes*. https://www.forbes.com/sites/robertamatuson/2022/10/04/the-attraction-of-subtraction-why-less-means-more-productivity/

Mitchell, T. D. (2007). *Critical service-learning as social justice education*. University of Wisconsin-Whitewater. https://www.uww.edu/documents/ce/6.credentilas_partneringDoc/cbl/Website/Critical-Service-Learning-as-Social-Justice-Education.pdf

Montessori, M. (1967). *The absorbent mind*. Henry Holt.

Moosalamoo Center. (n.d.). Moosalamoo Center. https://sites.google.com/a/rnesu.org/moosalamoo-center/

Murphy, E. R. (2023). Hope and well-being. *Current Opinion in Psychology, 50,* 101558. https://doi.org/10.1016/j.copsyc.2023.101558

Murray, D. W., Rosanbalm, K. D., Christopoulos, C., & Hamoudi, A. (2015). *Self-regulation and toxic stress: Foundations for understanding self-regulation from an applied developmental perspective*. OPRE Report #2015-21. Office of Planning, Research and Evaluation, Administration for Children and Families, U.S. Department of Health and Human Services.

Nagoski, E., & Nagoski, A. (2019). *Burnout: The secret to unlocking the stress cycle*. Ballantine Books.

Noddings, N. (1984). *Caring: A feminine approach to ethics and moral education*. University of California Press.

Occupational Therapy for Children Group (OTFC). (n.d.). *What is co-regulation?* https://otfcgroup.com.au/what-is-co-regulation/

PBLWorks. (n.d.). What is PBL? Retrieved November 30, 2024, from https://www.pblworks.org/what-is-pbl

Price, D. (2021). *Laziness does not exist*. Simon and Schuster.

Quintanilla, D. (2023, September 28). Maintaining your core values as a teacher. *Edutopia*. https://www.edutopia.org/article/maintaining-your-core-values-teacher/

Riener, M., & Willingham, D. (2010). The myth of learning styles. *Change: The Magazine of Higher Learning*, 42(5), 32–35. https://doi.org/10.1080/00091383.2010.503139

Roepke, A. M., Jayawickreme, E., & Riffle, O. M. (2014). Meaning and health: A systematic review. *Applied Psychology: Health and Well-Being*, 6(3), 341–364. https://doi.org/10.1111/aphw.12048

Rogers, C. R. (1951). *Client-centered therapy: Its current practice, implications, and theory, with chapters*. Houghton Mifflin.

Runyan, C. (2021, March 25). On healing our distressed nervous systems. *The On Being Project*. https://onbeing.org/programs/christine-runyan-on-healing-our-distressed-nervous-systems

Schorling, J. (2024). *The space between stimulus and response*. University of Virginia School of Medicine, Mindfulness Matters, Blog Post. March 4.

Semin, G. R., & Cacioppo, J. T. (2014). You are in sync with me: Neural correlates of interpersonal synchrony with a partner. *Neuroscience*, 277, 842–858. https://doi.org/10.1016/j.neuroscience.2014.07.051

Shanks, M. (n.d.). *An introduction to design thinking process guide*. Stanford University. https://web.stanford.edu/~mshanks/MichaelShanks/files/509554.pdf

Singh, P. (2024). *Teacher Roles in Personalized Learning*. LinkedIn. https://www.linkedin.com/posts/katy-farber-1a8a256_impactful-personalised-learning-that-empowers-activity-7254195077844029441-jzzV?utm_source=share&utm_medium=member_desktop&rcm=ACoAAAE4HNABsIhqiVj-D4Rmh8LDupmnErov8PPo

Sobel, D. (2004). *Place-based education: Connecting classrooms and communities*. The Orion Society.

Spelic, S. (2017, December 28). Letting go of school in order to think about education. *Medium*. https://medium.com/identity-education-and-power/letting-go-of-school-in-order-to-think-about-education-f9e3fb0878d8

Stanford, L. (2022, August 25). Most parents don't want their kids to become teachers, poll finds. *EdWeek*. https://www.edweek.org/teaching-learning/most-parents-dont-want-their-kids-to-become-teachers-poll-finds/2022/08

Substance Abuse and Mental Health Services Administration. (2023, September 21). *Biden-Harris Administration awards grants to expand Certified Community Behavioral Health Clinics across United States*. U.S. Department of Health and Human Services. https://www.samhsa.gov/newsroom/press-announcements/20230921/biden-harris-administration-awards-grants-to-expand-certified-community-behavioral-health-clinics-across-united-states#:~:text=The%20Community%20Mental%20Health%20Act%20of%201963%2C%20passed%20as%20part,care%20available%20in%20the%20community.

Tarrant Institute for Innovative Education. (n.d.). What is proficiency-based education? University of Vermont. https://tiie.w3.uvm.edu/blog/proficiency-based-education/#.YXbSE9nMLt0

Thomas, L., Rienties, B., Tuytens, M., Devos, G., Kelchtermans, G., & Vanderlinde, R. (2021). Unpacking the dynamics of collegial networks in relation to beginning teachers' job attitudes. *Research Papers in Education, 36*(5), 611–636. https://doi.org/10.1080/02671522.2020.1736614

The Trevor Project. (2021, August 19). *LGBTQ youth suicide prevention in schools.* The Trevor Project. https://www.thetrevorproject.org/research-briefs/lgbtq-youth-suicide-prevention-in-schools/

Turnaround for Children. (n.d.). *Whole-child design blueprint.* Turnaround for Children. https://turnaroundusa.org/toolbox/wcdesign/

Vedantam, S. (Host). (2023, July 31). You 2.0: Fighting despair [Audio podcast episode]. In *Hidden Brain.* Hidden Brain Media. https://hiddenbrain.org/podcast/you-2-0-fighting-despair/

Venet, A. S. (2023). *Equity-centered trauma-informed education.* Routledge.

Vermont Association for Middle Level Education (VAMLE). (n.d.). *Middle school is not a building.* Vermont Association for Middle Level Education. https://www.vamle.org/middle-school-is-not-a-building/

Walters, E. A. (2024, August 9). Teaching physics with a real-world context. *Edutopia.* https://www.edutopia.org/article/real-world-physics-project

Warren, J. (n.d.). Daily trip with Jeff Warren. In *Calm* [Audio]. https://www.calm.com

Web MD. (2022). What is compassion fatigue? https://www.webmd.com

Will, M., & Najarro, I. (2023, March 24). What is culturally responsive teaching? *Education Week.* https://www.edweek.org/teaching-learning/culturally-responsive-teaching-culturally-responsive-pedagogy/2022/04

Willis, J. (2007). *Brain-friendly strategies for the inclusion classroom.* Paul H. Brookes Publishing.

Winfrey, O. (2013.). Brené Brown on the 3 things you can do to stop a shame spiral [Video]. *Oprah.com.* https://www.oprah.com/oprahs-lifeclass/brene-brown-on-the-3-things-you-can-do-to-stop-a-shame-spiral-video#:~:text=If%20you're%20caught%20in,trust%2C%20and%20telling%20your%20story.

Xavier University Library. (n.d.). *Makerspace for education.* Xavier University. Retrieved November 5, 2024, from https://libguides.xavier.edu/makerspace/foreducation

For Product Safety Concerns and Information please contact our EU
representative GPSR@taylorandfrancis.com
Taylor & Francis Verlag GmbH, Kaufingerstraße 24, 80331 München, Germany

www.ingramcontent.com/pod-product-compliance
Lightning Source LLC
Chambersburg PA
CBHW060315240426
43661CB00059B/2775